Blind Dogs & S

CH01337691

Book production in Reno, NV (USA)
by Peartree Books LLC (www.peartreebooks.com)

Copy-edited by Kate Nascimento (kneditorial.com)

Cover designed by Chamara Cruzz (cruzzcreation)

DEDICATION

Dedicated to Blackie and his "sisters," past and present, who accompanied us on Blackie's journey in darkness: Angel, Jazmine, Brownie, Princess, and Olivia.

All profits from the sale of this book go to local dog rescue charities. For more information, including how you can help or adopt a dog in need of rescue in Hong Kong, go to: www.hongkongdogrescue.com.

CONTENTS

BLIND DOGS & SEEING EYE HUMANS

INTRODUCTION

Consider for a moment that it's tomorrow morning and you're asleep in the comfort of your bed. The sound of your smartphone alarm startles you, seeming to come way too early as it does every day. You go to reach for it in the darkness, but you can't see it. In fact, the darkness is so still that even the little illumination that's usually there is absent.

You search for the sound of the irritating alarm and eventually find it, then struggle as your fingers search for what yesterday seemed like an easy-to-find button that turns it off. It's something you've done nearly every day and yet, this morning, it seems nearly impossible. As the sound of the alarm disappears, you blink your eyes repeatedly trying to wake up. Still nothing, not even a glimmer of light. A thought races quickly across your mind: I'm blind!

This is our rescue dog Blackie's story (absent the smartphone). He woke up one day in November 2017 and was suddenly blind, the victim of Sudden Acquired Retinal Degeneration Syndrome ("SARDS"). Sadly, we didn't understand he was blind for about six weeks afterward, when he was formally diagnosed with SARDS—a disease in dogs causing sudden and permanent, but not life-threatening nor painful, blindness[1]. I was doubly heartbroken, once for his going blind and again for it taking six weeks to realize it, since dogs can't tell us what they're going through. Reality hit: It was time to rescue Blackie again.

---

[1] For more information on SARDS see Wikipedia (wikipedia.org/wiki/Sudden_acquired_retinal_degeneration_syndrome).

This book shares the knowledge I've gained since then about caring for a blind dog, in the hope that others can learn and benefit from my experiences. I share these learning experiences that we went through together in my "Tips from Blackie's journey" throughout this book, and an index to these 30 tips is provided in Appendix D. Blackie's blindness gave me a chance to be his "seeing eye human," a respectable purpose in life. Whether your dog contracted SARDS or became blind less suddenly, or if you're considering adopting a blind dog, you can learn to unconditionally love your best friend even more by becoming his seeing eye human too.

You'll need to make some changes; nothing too drastic, but the little things matter. You'll be amazed and inspired by your blind buddy and his will to continue to live life to its fullest, which I can only imagine is the opposite of the despair and hopelessness many of us humans would feel if we suddenly became blind.

Wherever you and your little guy may be on his journey, I hope this book will help you find the light to keep him shining. Yes, I refer to "him" throughout this book, but the lessons are identical if your buddy is actually a "her" (or even a cat perhaps), and whether they are recently blind, nearing blindness, or have been blind for quite some time.

Thank you for picking up this book and congratulations on beginning or continuing your journey of unconditional love with your own blind dog.

I hope that Blackie's story will help you to better appreciate the day-to-day challenges your own blind dog may be struggling with. While I don't dwell on it in the main body of this book, which is focused on loving and caring for a blind dog, I will briefly mention that we had to rescue Blackie again about eight months after he became blind, when a traumatic head injury left him temporarily paralyzed and a candidate for euthanasia. I hadn't considered euthanasia when he contracted SARDS, and wouldn't consider it for his paralysis. ***No way!*** Thankfully Blackie beat the odds stacked against him through love, caring, and, most notably, acupuncture. His resilient spirit rescued me again by providing me with a purpose in life, to accompany him on yet another journey to recovery.

Tragedy recently struck again, about a year and a half after overcoming his paralysis, when in August 2020, he was diagnosed with Stage 4 kidney disease. The vets gave him one to two weeks to live with the suggestion that we "put him to sleep.". *No way!* Not for this warrior! As I began to write this book nearly two months later, Blackie was still alive, albeit with a diminished capacity for day-to-day activities, but again rescuing me with a purposeful life. Sadly, Blackie passed away just as the first draft of this book was finished. You can read more about Blackie in Appendix B.

Finally, as you turn these pages and confidently absorb insights about caring for and unconditionally loving your blind dog, also thank yourself for helping

600+ abandoned dogs in need of rescue at Hong Kong Dog Rescue ("HKDR"), the truly no-kill dog rescue operation in Hong Kong.

All profits from the sale of this book go to HKDR and other local dog rescue charities. For more information, including how you can help or adopt a dog in need of rescue in Hong Kong, go to: www.hongkongdogrescue.com.

1 BLIND BUT STILL MY BEST FRIEND

Man's best friend ... or dog's best friend?

That common phrase so often used by us humans to describe the bond between a dog and his owner (which could be either a man or a woman). I often wonder whether dogs would have a similar phrase that refers to us as "dog's best friend"?

Fortunately, I know the term "best friend" can also refer to a family member, such as when a daughter says that her mom is her best friend. This is important to me because I have always thought of my dogs as family, and as best friends.

All of us have experienced a family member becoming ill and asking for a little assistance, whether it's to make some honey and lemon tea or perhaps take them to an urgent care clinic. Many of us have also experienced a close friend going through some difficult times and talking to us about it, perhaps to complain or vent but also to ask for help. In both cases, our human nature is to listen and help in whatever way we can.

The challenge with our dogs is twofold. First, despite being family and our best friend, they aren't equipped with the power of speech to tell us what's on their minds, what's bothering them, or how we may be able to help. Second, their entire being is usually centered around us—they don't have television shows to watch, or smartphones or tablets to occupy them. How many of us have dogs that just mope around the house when we're too busy to play with them? We have work, we have other friends to spend time with, we have family to take care of … yet all they have is us. We are the center of their being.

So when they aren't feeling well, we usually identify it through signs of a behavior or character change that may, at first, be small. We try to judge their character when they're healthy and happy, and draw on this to assess when they may not be so well or have become unhealthy. Unfortunately, we don't always get it right, or it takes us too long to figure it out. Why?

While perhaps in part it's because we don't watch them every minute of the day, it's primarily because of their inability to tell us what's on their mind. Ironically, it's often said that dogs are the best judge of a person's character. I surmise that this is the combination of our dog being totally centered around us, watching our every move and action, and listening acutely to what we say and how we say it. Sure, they may not understand it all, but those verbal cues— speaking softly at times while raising our voice at others, or having less energy and enthusiasm in our tones when we speak—are interpreted by them as signs of our demeanor and whether we're feeling happy, healthy, depressed, or ill. Add to this that, at least in my own case, we often tell them what we're feeling (e.g., "Sorry buddy, but I have a headache and I don't feel like walking tonight"). All of this shapes them into an unbelievably strong judge of our character. I truly believe that my dogs know when I'm not feeling well based on my character, regardless of whether or not I tell them.

In hindsight, when the vet confirmed on a day in January 2018 that Blackie had suffered permanent blindness perhaps as much as six weeks earlier, I felt a huge burden because I had misjudged his character. I knew it wouldn't take Blackie six weeks to work out if I wasn't feeling well. But with that burden I was able to reconsider what Blackie's new needs were—and there were many—in order to preserve a good quality of life. At the top of the list was that he needed me.

He needed his best friend (that's me) to assist him on his new journey. He needed me not to love him less, as I'm sure dogs and most other animals subscribe to the theory that only the strong survive, and recognizing his own blindness had to make him feel weak and vulnerable. I had heard stories through my work with HKDR that many owners consider abandonment or even euthanasia when their dog becomes blind. This is ridiculous and, in my view, sinful. I have two words to say to this: *NO WAY!*

Blackie needed my help, and that of my entire household. Sure, it took him a couple of years to accept me when our lives first came together, but we became best pals. I had gained his total trust and at that time, more than ever, he wanted to trust me to take care of him. I couldn't let him down. He looked up to me as his best friend and—blind or not blind— he was ***still my best friend***.

It's incredibly important for any dog owner to consider this and reassess what it means for their dog caretaking responsibilities. A blind dog can live a happy life if they have the right support, love, and an environment that accommodates their new needs. When you can give this to them, their character doesn't change, but their ***total trust*** in you grows immensely. And you grow as well.

In the following chapters, I will walk you through the importance of understanding and accepting your dog's blindness—for both you and your dog—before delving into what I call "The Magical Eight Modifiers" of living with, and loving, a blind dog.

2 UNDERSTANDING BLINDNESS

Total darkness

I want to shed some light on the total darkness that is blindness, through a brief discussion of the causes and effects of your dog being blind. I also address several of the misguided perceptions associated with blind dogs to separate fact from fiction. I do not specifically discuss the concept of impaired partial vision, although one would think that many of the topics discussed herein also apply in that case, particularly if the impairment is reasonably expected to deteriorate into full blindness.

Before we start, rest assured that your blind dog can be a better companion and best friend than some sighted dogs.

Causes

At the most basic level, blindness in dogs is similar to that in humans and may be something they're born with, the result of an accident, or something that develops over time due to diseases and aging. As for diseases and aging, common reasons include cataracts, glaucoma, diabetes-related diseases, and retinal diseases. While in many of these cases, blindness occurs progressively over a period of time (particularly with aging dogs and certain breeds and sexes, which may be more susceptible), sudden blindness is generally the result of SARDS (as in Blackie's case), a disease resulting in the removal of an eye, or an accident. I have also heard many stories where a dog initially had a cataract or glaucoma in one eye, and the same issue eventually also occurred in the other eye.

For the progressive diseases, early detection, monitoring, and possible treatments are important to delay the onset of blindness. You should take a diagnosis of these eye diseases as seriously as you would with any other family member. While I do recognize the potential for expensive costs associated with early treatment and prevention, it is important also to recognize that delaying such treatments often results in higher costs later on, as well as the heavier emotional burden you may bear for not treating it earlier.

This is not a textbook on veterinary ophthalmology, so you won't find much more of a medical or technical assessment of these causes herein. However, I do strongly recommend that if your dog is diagnosed with the early onset of any eye disease, you seek out a veterinary ophthalmologist for a specialized consultation. You wouldn't expect a loved one with a specific condition only to receive advice from a family physician, so treat your dog just like any other family member. In my experience, the cost of a visit is well worth what you can learn about loving and caring for your dog as the disease progresses. It may also result in a rather inexpensive treatment to prevent (or at least delay) the onset of blindness. In the case of my youngest dog, Princess, who suffers from dry eyes as a result of the inability to regularly produce natural tears, we have to administer inexpensive eye drops to her three to five times each day. If this wasn't detected early and treated regularly, Princess would have gone blind years ago.

Effects

No matter the cause, the effects of blindness in dogs are very similar, although dogs that lose their vision gradually usually adjust better than those with sudden or rapid loss.

The principal effect of blindness is that your dog will need to adapt in order to perform daily tasks and preserve their quality of life. Dogs are usually very resilient and adapt much more quickly than humans. This is probably, in part, due to their character and the fact that they have so much less to focus on than us humans do. After all, blindness will not affect their ability to go to work, watch television, use a smartphone or tablet, and so on.

However, there are several important reasons they adapt more quickly than humans. Firstly, and perhaps the most important, is that they have us to assist them and be their seeing eye human.

Secondly, dogs have incredibly heightened senses of smelling and hearing in comparison to us humans. Actually, sighted dogs can also see much further than humans and better at night, although the ability to distinguish colors may be less acute. However, the sense of sight is lost when they are blind so that they become more reliant on those other primary senses of smelling and hearing, which are so much more acute than in humans. This is why certain breeds are trained as detection dogs for narcotics, explosives, human remains (cadavers), and more. Not all breeds are the same in terms of how acute these senses are, which is why we often see only a few particular breeds at an airport as drug sniffers. However, all dogs' sense of smell is significantly stronger than those of humans.

So too are dogs' ears. Dogs are able to register sounds of 35,000 vibrations per second (compared to 20,000 per second in humans), and they can also shut off their inner ear in order to filter out distracting sounds[2].

When a dog is blind, these two senses kick in to compensate for the lack of sight. As a result, their primary sense of smell effectively becomes their eyes, in terms of how they find things. Dogs remember specific scents for a very long period of time and are able to associate scents with specific people, places, objects, etc. I sometimes run into someone that looks familiar, but I can't remember what their name is or be sure that I have indeed met them before. Dogs, on the other hand, stroll on up, sniff another dog's rear end, and immediately remember whether they've met before (names are of no importance to them!).

---

[2] Source: Britannica.com (britannica.com/animal/dog/senses).

A dog's sense of hearing plays a similarly important role, although in my own experience their hearing is an alert mechanism principally directed at helping them navigate in a certain direction or toward a specific location, and then their sniffer kicks in to get them more precisely where they want to be. Many times when I walk my Princess, who isn't blind but tends to wander off (I never walk her on a leash), I will yell toward her, "Princess!" and she immediately stops and looks in my direction. The only difference with my blind dog Blackie is that his hearing is now always switched on to correct for the lack of vision, seemingly listening to each and every sound out there. He actually wanders very little (in contrast to Princess) as he's always listening for my footsteps or the sound of my voice to guide him. This behavior isn't unusual with blind dogs, and many owners describe them as being more attentive.

The combined effect of a blind dog using their senses of hearing and smell is "mapping" in their mind specific memories of the layout of places in their life, i.e., where they are and where they want to go. I discuss mapping later herein as I explore ways to improve your blind dog's quality of life at home and on walks.

What about their other senses, touch and taste? From a practical standpoint, there's no difference between a blind dog's senses of touch and taste and those of a sighted dog. Generally speaking, a dogs' sense of touch is also a primary sense, and a blind dog still touches people and things, but probably works harder to associate the smell of what they are touching as a memory they catalog into their mind. As for taste, a blind dog will continue to have the same undiscerning taste buds they had before going blind.

Another reason dogs can adapt to blindness better than us humans is that they have an exploratory nature that, when combined with their other senses, simply keeps them ready to explore. I have heard a story of a fire department's dog named Sarge that was trained to detect explosives and suddenly went blind, unbeknownst to his firemen handlers. Sarge continued to be dragged around at fire scenes searching with his heightened sense of smell for explosives despite being blind. As a result, it took some time for the fire department crew to realize that Sarge had gone blind.

Many blind dogs, particularly those that suddenly go blind with SARDS, will exhibit a heightened hunger level, but this has no correlation to their sense of taste. Their animal survival instincts will kick in and their appetite will seem to have increased as they effectively *fear* not knowing when they will eat next. It is analogous to a bear loading up on food before settling in for the winter hibernation.

A cautionary note here not to give in to that heightened hunger level, as many owners describe how their dogs gained weight after becoming blind. You can still give them those extra treats or table scraps in moderation, but keep it in check, especially as blind dogs inevitably become slightly-to-significantly less active than sighted dogs. This lower activity level is the indirect result of their anxiety associated with the loss of sight. In my experience, this reduced activity level is most pronounced early in their blindness and as they get more confident moving around, in part by using you as their seeing eye human, their activity levels can often increase, but still not to a level comparable to that of a sighted dog. A blind dog's owner needs to recognize this more sedentary lifestyle and consider the appropriate modifications to a blind dog's diet and nutrition, which I will discuss further in Chapter 13 on Aging.

Another personal example of how anxiety can affect a blind dog's behavior is that Blackie has effectively become our home security system since going blind. When he could see, he hardly ever cared when someone came to our door (assuming, of course, that he knew I was already at home) and left it to another member of the pack to bark and alert the household. Nowadays, he seems to hear the arrival before the doorbell is even rung, and barks like a junkyard dog a few seconds before we find out why.

These principal effects of blindness—heightened senses of hearing and smell coupled with heightened anxiety—are guide posts you need to focus on, as they will help you gauge how your blind dog is doing at any time, in any place. And this brings us to the last effect: Trust becomes wobbly.

Your best friend trusted you before and will continue to trust you. However, there will be (perhaps many) times when it looks like he doesn't trust you or other family members. The truth is that it's only wobbly as he learns what trust means in the darkness of being blind. The best example I can give builds further on the heightened hunger level that you'll observe. It is temporary and as he gets more confident that you will continue to feed him regularly (or in the case of my home, that he is being fed equally with the rest of the pack), the anxiety around his trust level will gradually go away. This is only one example, and you may observe many.

I often say to my dogs—Blackie and the others—"*total trust*." I want them to know they can trust me, but it's a frequent reminder to myself that my dog wants and needs to trust me, as I'm the center of their world. No one should forget this. Give your dogs, blind and sighted, that total trust.

Separating fact from fiction

A discussion about understanding blindness would be incomplete without separating fact from fiction. In simple terms, the facts are that a blind dog is as great a companion or best friend as a dog with sight, and their ability to love unconditionally can only become stronger as you assume the role of his seeing eye human.

I am disgusted when I hear that an owner euthanized or abandoned a blind dog. Would you euthanize a family member who loses their vision? The excuses have included:

- Blind dogs have a poor quality of life → Not true
- Blind dogs generally require a lot more attention → Not true[3]

---

[3] Admittedly, blind dogs require some attention to modify their behaviors when they first become blind, but thereafter they

- Blind dogs can't be trained → Not true
- Blind dogs cost more → Not true
- Blind dogs can't guard your house → Not true
- It's depressing to spend time with them → Not true

I think this pretty much sums it all up.

Interestingly, the same list of fictional excuses above is often cited as a reason not to rescue and adopt a blind dog. Again, none of these excuses are based on fact. However, I do appreciate that when it comes to welcoming a new member into the family, our human nature is to want that member to at least be healthy when they join our family. This is reasonable and something I do not begrudge. Anyone rescuing and adopting any dog has to have that feel-good factor in their heart from day one, the feeling that you and the dog were meant to be. But a big call out to those owners who have rescued and adopted a blind dog: **Bless your heart!**

---

don't require much more attention than dogs that have their sight.

3 ACCEPTANCE BY YOU

Blind dogs see with their hearts

I first heard this phrase from a business acquaintance whose wife had adopted a blind dog when she was studying veterinary ophthalmology. I remember researching it at the time and couldn't identify where it had originated, but I've had no difficulty validating how accurate it is. In my case, Blackie sees with his heart as part of the "total trust" relationship we have. And the payoff for me is both in having a great companion and being his seeing eye human.

Your ability to accept your blind dog's challenges is the first building block in creating the right environment for him to enjoy a good quality of life. If you have difficulty accepting it, he will have even more difficulty.

It begins with opening your heart. He needs you. Begin to judge him on what he can do, rather than what he can't.

Eliminate pity and create dignity! You can't change his misfortune, but you can create the home and household environment that gives him dignity. I first learned the phrase "living with dignity" years before Blackie became blind, and it was attributed to how to provide loving support to an elderly relative with Alzheimer's. But it is equally applicable to how you support your blind dog. When you give him dignity, it has a tremendous impact on his confidence level, helping him to overcome the challenges of constant darkness. There will be more on building his confidence and the "Magical Eight Modifiers" later in the book.

Our dogs tend to mirror many of our emotions, or at least they feed off of them. When we're excited to go for a walk, they too become excited. Create a positive atmosphere that allows your blind dog to be positive. There's no place for pity, only for those positive contributions you make to allow him to live with dignity.

Make time to adjust

Unless your dog becomes blind in an accident or operation, or is stricken with SARDS, which gave my Blackie his sudden, immediate, and permanent blindness, you will hopefully have some time to adjust. Regardless of whether your dog's blindness is sudden or gradual, you can start implementing the "Magical Eight Modifiers" (discussed later herein) immediately. However, your dog will need some time to learn how to live as a blind dog and you will need some time to remember how much he needs your help and guidance through that learning curve. Remember, you are his seeing eye human.

Dogs learn quite quickly especially when it involves routine activities and even more so if rewards are involved. Recalling Pavlov's theory, in which dogs were trained quickly to recognize that the sound of a bell meant food was coming, you will see your blind dog learn and adapt quickly to his new norms. And you should give him those rewards, but not too many treats as dogs also feast on enthusiastic praise as a reward. In the case of blind dogs that rely on their sense of hearing, your positive praise means so much more to them than it may to a sighted dog.

A reasonable period of time to adjust is about one to three months. This isn't a very long time to us humans, but do remember that it equates to about eight to twenty-one months in dog years.

Dealing with depression

It's natural to feel a bit depressed, especially when you see your blind dog full of anxiety or having difficulties with daily activities. Similar to pity, you will need to suppress those feelings and open your heart, continuing to share your positive energy and emotions with your blind dog. Harry Houdini, the famed magician, supposedly once said, "Keep up your enthusiasm! There is nothing more contagious than exuberant enthusiasm." This is certainly the case when it comes to how you interact with your blind dog.

Open your eyes

You have the ***superpower of observation***, and you will need to use it all the time. Watching your blind dog doing everything during that early adaptation period is especially crucial. This superpower of observation will lead you to understand what he needs your help with, or what you may need to modify to make it a little easier for him.

Let me start setting the stage by sharing some experiences from my journey with Blackie:

Tips from Blackie's journey: The slightest sounds

Early in his journey, I observed Blackie when he went to drink from his water bowl. He knew where it was; it had been in the same place in the house for years, at the end of a narrow hall near the kitchen area. While observing him, I noticed that his normal drinking position was that he kept his rear end toward the rest of the house. When there was the slightest sound, he would jerk his head around quickly and remain in a listening pose for a bit while he tried to figure out what the sound was. I could see his anxiety, given his reliance on his sense of hearing but being unable to see what it was. I soon also observed that his drinking routine could stop quickly when there were frequent interruptions to this otherwise simple task. An easy fix turned out to be to relocate the water bowl to a more open area that didn't make him feel trapped in a narrow hallway with his back to all the sounds.

Tips from Blackie's journey: Show a little dignity

Another example was observing how the rest of the pack dealt with Blackie. Interestingly, the two older dogs (Brownie and Jazmine) were quick to give Blackie some dignity, often getting out of his way if he plodded toward them. However, Angel and Princess were less accommodating, presumably because it took them much longer to understand what Blackie was dealing with. As a result, observing when Blackie would move around became important so that I could alert Angel or Princess to "be nice" in order to avoid any confrontations. Eventually Angel and Princess also learned to adapt. They, too, just needed time to adjust to Blackie's new norms.

Do not take your superpower of observation lightly since he relies on you, as his seeing eye human, to observe and act on the things that he can't or that affect his quality of life.

Reflect on major life changes

It's awesome that one of your life decisions was to care for a blind dog. Bless your heart.

As your blind dog's seeing eye human, you should pause to consider how any big decisions you make in the future may affect your blind companion. This is not to say that having a blind dog should cause you to change those decisions, but rather just that you should consider how he may need a little assistance to adapt to your changes. Remember, dogs love routines but do adapt quickly. Blind dogs, however, with their primary senses of hearing and smell, just need that little extra consideration when life throws new changes at them.

I won't ponder a long list of possible life changes, but the short list below is worthwhile. Keep in mind that none of these require any burden as you continue to provide your unconditional love to, and the best quality of life for, your best friend.

The members of your household change

Maybe you're getting married, or perhaps a baby has come along. Have you ever watched a YouTube video when parents bring home a baby and their dog's curiosity is (usually) exciting? You get the impression that the dog is trying to figure out who the new member of the household is. When you watch these types of videos, you can appreciate that the dog is leading with his sense of sight: he *sees* the new family member. When it's a baby, the dog very cautiously gets nearer and nearer the small being, and then starts to sniff the baby, wanting to know the scent of this new household member. Similarly, when the new household member is an adult, the dog is usually more apprehensive, as he sees the adult as a much larger figure, but nevertheless approaches with the same desire to know the scent of this new household member.

The point here is that your blind dog cannot lead with a sense of sight and will therefore be more apprehensive with any new family member, small or big. This initial socializing and bonding experience will take longer as he first tries to understand the sound of the new household member's voice, often judging the person on their volume, tone, and what they say. Once your blind dog starts to get past the sound of their voice, then it's time to understand the scent of the new person. With a newborn baby, often there is no sound (other than perhaps crying) that your blind dog can first associate with the new member of the household. And understanding a newborn's scent can be a challenge as you may, at first, try to keep some safe distance between your dog and baby. I won't even get into how some dogs eventually experience some jealousy when you may be focusing more of your time on that new person, rather than your four-legged buddy.

All of this requires a little more time so that your blind dog can learn to trust that new household member through sounds and scents. Work with your dog so that he hears and smells—since he can't see—that the new person is welcome and here for good. Encourage initial contact between them to be slow and cautious; rewards help. Some dogs, such as my Angel (may she rest in peace), loved when friends were visiting and asked for her paw. She would light up because the person knew she had a behavior to show them. However, my blind Blackie, who loves to give me his paw, will never lift his paw for visitors (let alone a new household member) and has a defensive "no way" look on his face when someone asks.

Just remember how your blind dog leads with his hearing and smell, and use these as creative tools in early interactions to help your blind dog get to know and accept the new household member.

On the flip side, your household may experience the loss of a family member, perhaps through divorce or a child moving away to college (we will not get into a household member's death, which is a whole other topic on how dogs grieve their lost companions). The absence of a household member, particularly one who is close to your blind dog, can again cause depression in your dog, even if he is not blind. The simple solution is for you to notice this with your superpower of observation and try to give him a little more attention when appropriate. The key difference with a blind dog, however, is that he does not "see" the person is gone, he just no longer hears or smells the person on a daily basis. The practical solution is to observe and recognize the gap that the person's absence will cause in your blind dog's routine. For example, if the person used to do the daily morning ritual dog walk, you will need to fill the gaps since your blind dog, while likely to be depressed about the person being gone, takes comfort in routine.

You change jobs or start to have prolonged absences

I am convinced that when someone changes their job, dogs can tell. They may see that you have a different daily routine or may sense a different attitude in you before and after work. My Angel (may she rest in peace) knew rather quickly when I retired as I was suddenly home every day, which meant more time for her. In fact, because she knew I was home and no longer saw me leaving the house nearly every week with a suitcase packed for business travel, she began refusing to walk with other household members and would instead just wait until I would take her out. Dogs know when your work routine changes.

And perhaps your new work requires travel, resulting in prolonged absences away from your dog and yet another change to your dog's routine.

Remember that your dog loves routine and when you change it, they feel it. And when the routine means less of your time, there's a little bit of heartbreak felt by your blind dog (after all, they lead with their hearts). You should consider how these changes affect your blind dog and whether it merely means that you need to give them a little more of your attention before you leave and after you return home. We have been fortunate to have a pack at the house, as the companionship that my Blackie gets from his "sisters" keeps his mind occupied when my routine changes.

Other unexpected changes

"Expect the unexpected": a phrase I heard a lot over the years, particularly while training in the United States Marine Corps. Unfortunately, dogs don't do this, regardless of whether they have full vision or are blind. Thus, it's helpful to your little buddy to consider how he reacts or will react to sudden unexpected changes.

An example that a friend recently shared with me was the direct result of the COVID-19 pandemic in 2020. His employer had instituted workplace changes whereby he initially started "working from home" every other day. His dog loved that he was at home more often and, admittedly, my friend loved being able to take his coffee breaks with a little dog-loving time. After a short period, his employer changed the policy such that he was instructed to work from home as much as possible, only going into his place of work when absolutely required. He and his dog loved this period of time as "daddy" seemed to be home nearly every day. Routines had changed, but because of the increased companion time, both he and his dog were living the dream.

Unfortunately, it was time to wake up when the number of COVID-19 cases had dropped and my friend was suddenly required to be back in the workplace on a daily basis. He noticed immediately that his dog seemed depressed when he was once again preparing to leave for work in the mornings and a bit surprised when he came home in the evening (with that "where have you been?" attitude). Dogs just simply love routines and this unexpected change in the routine of my friend, who had been home nearly daily for a few months and was suddenly not at home most of the day, did not sit well with his dog. My friend recognized this immediately (he also did not like the thought of being away from his dog again on a daily basis) and did two things. First—the obvious—he made his morning pre-work time and evening post-work time more focused on interacting with his dog. Second, which I thought was quite innovative, he set reminders on his smartphone throughout the day to access his Alexa virtual assistant device at home via an app on his phone and instruct it to say something to his dog using his dog's name. When I questioned how it helped his dog, given that whatever Alexa said was in Alexa's voice rather than his own, he confessed that while he hoped that his dog was reacting to the sound of his name, it may have been more therapeutic for my friend having those few minutes throughout the day just to interact with his little buddy from far away.

The author and Blackie both wearing "muzzles" during a vet visit in light of the vet's COVID-19 mask-wearing guidelines

Your own life will throw unexpected changes at you. Just keep in mind how those changes may affect your dog's routine and whether there's anything you can do to ease the surprise, and often the anxiety, it may bring.

Final thoughts

Never forget that your blind dog sees with his heart, and you are his seeing eye human. It's easy for you to accept them when your heart is open and you actively use your superpower of observation to consider what's best for him. The tips provided in "The Magical Eight Modifiers" later herein will help.

4 ACCEPTANCE BY YOUR DOG

Acceptance comes easier to those without regrets

A common problem with us humans is that we have too many regrets. We feel remorse when things don't go well. Dogs generally have no feelings of regret, except perhaps those few times you may have helped him realize that your new pair of shoes was not a chew toy.

We, as humans, also tend to fixate on how to change things, and particularly how we can reverse or "fix" something that has gone badly. We can learn so much from watching dogs, as they do not dwell on the unchangeable and instead look forward to what is next, hoping it is an activity they enjoy, the company of a loved one, or, yes, a reward.

As such, the resilience dogs exhibit in combating disease is inspiring. They become a warrior for their own cause, looking forward while also trying to keep the special bond they have with you as bright as ever. And in the darkness that a blind dog experiences, that relationship with you becomes their brightness, their beacon of light.

The reason I discuss acceptance by *you* before acceptance by your dog is because your dog needs to know you have accepted his blindness, that you still love him unconditionally in the same way or even more, and that life goes on, albeit with necessary modifications. This is the foundation that your blind dog needs so that he can see you are his beacon of light and hope, and that, together, you will both continue the beautiful relationship that you have always had.

In the case of my Blackie, this was extremely pronounced, given the six-week period that he likely had been blind but it had gone undetected and misunderstood. Very quickly after I knew and accepted it, and started acting on the Magical Eight Modifiers (discussed later herein), it was clear that Blackie started to accept it as well. It didn't take long; he had no regrets and wanted to get on and never give up on himself, or me and my love for him.

I must admit that right after Blackie was diagnosed with SARDS, I re-read an inspirational book that I have read no less than ten times in my life. In *The Twelfth Angel* by author Og Mandino[4], a little boy suffering from an incurable disease repeatedly tells himself, "**Never Give Up!**" I felt that while Blackie's story was different, the positive spirit Blackie presented was just as inspirational as the little boy in the book. Blackie faces each day with his warrior spirit and positive outlook, and for this reason I'm proud to call him a hero, a term I usually reserve only

---

[4] Og Mandino has published many inspirational books, of which *The Twelfth Angel* is the author's favorite.

for those who have performed an astonishing act of valor[5].

Your blind dog will approach his life the same way. If he sees that you accept his blindness, he will as well. They look forward with excitement, not backward with regret.

What can you do to help him with his acceptance? There are a few key things at a very broad level before we get into the granular details of the Magical Eight Modifiers.

<u>Recognize depression</u>

Your superpower of observation must continue to be at work. Although your blind dog will be resilient,

---

[5] In the United States, the Medal of Honor is awarded to military personnel as the highest award for acts of valor. The majority of these medals are awarded posthumously. Living Medal of Honor recipients, of which there are few, go on with life allowing their inspiration to fuel that of others, both within and outside of the military. It is this infectious inspiration that Blackie has projected in the face of his adversity that has allowed the author to call Blackie a hero.

some depression is a normal reaction to the darkness they experience. Your blind dog will get past this, in particular by taking their emotional cues from you, but also based, in part, on what their life and character was before becoming blind.

In my Blackie's case, I could quickly recognize if a level of depression was coming over him. This meant it was time to play, or perhaps just have a nonsensical conversation with him. My job is to shield him from those feelings and implement a change that brings back that positive happy attitude.

Blackie also had the benefit of being in the household pack. The companionship of having those other dogs around has also helped, and his happiness is often re-engaged when he hears the others playing or being active. Each household composition is different in terms of the number of people and dogs, but simply engaging with your blind dog helps moments of depression or anxiety disappear like dust in the wind.

You aren't just his seeing eye human but also his antidepressant drug. Use your superpower of observation to know when another dosage is due.

Recognize dependency on other senses

I mention above that even nonsensical conversations help; the fact is, they help a lot. You must remember that blind dogs are highly dependent on their senses of hearing and smell. Having a conversation with your blind dog engages his sense of hearing and has such a positive impact on his quality of life as he understands your conversations with his heart.

Your recognition of the influence that sounds and smells have on your blind dog is a huge factor not just in dealing with the perception of depression, but in how you help him in every aspect of his quality of life. This applies when you're with him and could engage in a silly conversation, and even more so when you're not around. For example, what sounds is he likely to hear when you leave him alone at home? Remember that because they cannot see, they are more acutely tuned in to all sounds. In Blackie's case, we have come to leave some music or a television on as low-level background noise whenever nobody is at home so that he isn't frequently startled by other small sounds.

This awareness needs to extend to what sounds he hears even when you're with him inside or outside of his home. One example is when a friend joined me and Blackie on a walk. As usual, Blackie was attuned to whatever I was saying while also listening to other sounds. My friend received a call while we were walking and started talking on his phone for what was probably not more than four or five minutes. Even though I kept talking to Blackie as we walked, he was totally distracted by the sound of my friend having that phone conversation. I recognized this shortly into the call and, when the call ended, I politely established the "no phone calls while walking Blackie" rule. You will see this using your superpower of observation: sounds that seem ordinary to you and that you can drown out in your head because you are *looking* at something else, often become a challenge for blind dogs who are *listening* to everything around them.

In "The Magical Eight Modifiers", we will also discuss the need to remember that they're also trying to *smell* everything, allowing their minds to recall things through sound and scent. The best thing you can do is remember this high level of dependency they have on their other senses.

Help him to learn

In many respects, your blind dog will be learning everything all over again. You need to help him learn to live in his darkness, who and what to trust, and how to preserve his dignity as a blind dog. I personally have found that this didn't require much patience, but certainly resulted in even a stronger bond with my Blackie.

While there will be new things that he will need to learn, equal importance must be placed on how you help him re-learn the day-to-day things that can often be overlooked. Earlier I shared the example of how I had assumed he would continue to drink water as before, until my superpower of observation recognized his heightened sense of hearing was filtering other sounds and causing anxiety when he tried to drink. As you think about things he needs to learn, or re-learn, you must include activities such eating, drinking, urinating and defecating, visits to the vet (and hopefully a veterinary ophthalmologist), bathing, cleaning his teeth and ears, and so on.

And as you help him to re-learn these things, have a little patience, because he can't see what it is you want him to do. He's relying on those other senses and, of course, that "total trust" bond he has with you.

Final thoughts

Treat your blind dog with dignity as you help him overcome the challenges associated with being blind, and recognize the small things you can do to help him to accept his blindness. When this is done well, your blind dog will become not only your inspiration, but also one of your heroes.

5 THE MAGICAL EIGHT MODIFIERS

Abracadabra! And now for my next trick, I will make a blind dog see again

If only it were that simple. You have already accepted that your little buddy is blind and nothing is ever going to change that. He has also already accepted his new life of darkness, where you're the one that brings him light as his seeing eye human. It's now time to tackle how the two of you working together can ensure that his blindness will not hinder his day-to-day quality of life.

When I accompanied Blackie through the early steps of his journey in darkness, I realized that some of my behaviors and interactions as well as his normal activities had to be modified. When Blackie and I reached that point after two to three months where the "total trust" had been built on a new foundation, I reflected back on what the primary changes or modifications were that we had focused on. My list totaled eight broad categories and I thought, *this cannot be a coincidence.* We live in Hong Kong where the number eight is considered a lucky number (as it is across all of China). In the Chinese language, "eight" is pronounced as "ba", which sounds a lot like "fa", which translates into English directly as "fortune" but is loosely associated with being successful. There it was: Blackie and I were successful, having developed our Magical Eight Modifiers as summarized below:

Broad categories of the Magical Eight Modifiers
1.   Building confidence
2.   Simplify your home
3.   Old and new commands
4.   Simplify your walks
5.   Playtime
6.   Accessorizing helps
7.   Socializing
8.   Aging

While it's easy to summarize the places you went to at the end of a journey, the fact is that I couldn't have discovered many of these places without the help of others. I undertook relentless Internet research, intensive reading of other books on how to live with a blind dog[6], and endless (and still ongoing) discussions with friends, other dog lovers, and Blackie's veterinarians (in particular, his veterinary ophthalmologist). Through all this, I received a lot of pointers (no pun intended, if your blind dog is a Pointer) on things to do, observe, and consider modifying.

The order of the Magical Eight Modifiers is not random. Each of the modifiers builds from the successes achieved from those preceding them. "Building confidence," the first modifier, helps to strengthen your blind dog's total trust so the steps he takes throughout the journey seem easier. Please consider them in order, even if you're already far along your own journey and a particular modifier

---

[6] Refer to Appendix C: Other Resources, for some books about blind dogs that the author found very helpful.

category catches your attention. Many of the things that you can do cross over multiple modifiers—such as modifications in your home help to build your blind dog's confidence—so approaching these in the order presented is helpful.

Within each broad category, I'll give you tips that have been tried and tested with Blackie, and the resulting outcomes will be shared through my "Tips from Blackie's Journey". Admittedly those that I share are successful outcomes, as when I tried things that didn't work, we quickly pivoted in another direction on our journey. So quick were these pivots that I honestly can only remember one noteworthy failure: Blackie could not learn his left from his right.

Although I dedicate the focus of this book to living with blind dogs, it is worth mentioning that many of these modifiers are also worthwhile if you live with a one-eyed dog, as they too go through similar struggles of how to adjust to their day-to-day life.

And as magicians often say when they are about to show you something exciting … TA-DA! Let's dive into the Magical Eight Modifiers.

6 BUILDING CONFIDENCE

Confidence is a state of mind

This is no less true for your blind dog than it is for yourself. And your own confidence in life likely stems from feelings of being loved and safe, and having positive influences that contribute to you being happy with yourself and those around you.

There are some simple ways you can instill that confidence in your blind dog too.

Use of a bell

By now you've started to embrace your superpower of observation. But it's impossible to watch your blind dog every minute of the day. A small bell on his collar is a useful accessory that makes a sound and alerts you if he's moving. This can alert you day or night (if you're a light sleeper) that your blind dog is on the move and it's time to switch on your superpower.

Tips from Blackie's journey: Ding, ding, ding

We found the bell to be an unbelievably helpful aid for the first six months of Blackie's journey in darkness. The bell would result in us observing him and, in some instances, realizing that he needed some guidance. Fortunately, the bell never seemed to be a distraction for Blackie; he accepted it immediately. We also found it useful for the rest of our pack, as it alerted the other dogs to the fact that Blackie was on the move. I believe this was also useful at times when no humans were at home. Eventually, as Blackie became more comfortable and confident with his in-home movements, we discontinued the bell, which can get annoying for all involved.

Sounds and smells

In building your blind dog's confidence, conveying your affection to him is critical. He needs to know you're there; that your relationship is not impaired even if his vision is. To accomplish this, establish with yourself the importance of combining your superpower of observing him with your eyes with constantly also observing what he's hearing and smelling.

His minute-to-minute actions are the product of what he hears and smells, and his attempts to make sense of what is happening around him.

Tips from Blackie's journey: The water bowl location

I have already shared the water bowl example, but it's worthy of drawing upon again. By watching your dog in their daily actions, and wondering what he hears and smells that causes changes to those actions, you can identify things that need to be modified.

While helping him to modify his actions, the importance of rewards and praise can't be taken lightly. However, it's important not to just give him treats as these also serve his basic need to eat, which is associated with his less important sense of taste. The praise—"That's a good boy!"—said with gusto has the combined effect of touching his primary sense of hearing and creating that exuberant enthusiasm that, as Houdini said, is so contagious.

Tips from Blackie's journey: Praise, even for finding the water bowl

Continuing with Blackie's water bowl example, I found that praising him for finding his way to his new water bowl position both reinforced where it was located and seemed to make him more at ease drinking the water. He had confidence that the bowl was, in fact, filled with water, which has no scent, and not with something he should be scared of. This praise reinforced his behavior around a safe and necessary activity and helped give him more overall confidence.

His reliance on sound can be surprising, as us humans with good vision can easily drown out noises, particularly if we can see what causes them. As his seeing eye human, you need to talk to him more frequently and help him learn to follow the right sounds, such as your voice or that of another household member. Everyone should talk to him before touching him, to avoid startling him. And while talking to him, consider how other sounds may affect what he hears, or how competing sounds could cause him to become confused.

Tips from Blackie's journey: Muting competing sounds

We often have some music or a television playing in our home, a usually low background noise that can be pleasant for the entire pack when there's no other activity. I started to notice that when I called Blackie while that background noise existed, he often looked at me in a confused way. I experimented a few times and found that if I made the same effort while muting the television,

Blackie was both more attentive and didn't seem confused. As a result, he gradually increased his confidence levels in understanding what he was being asked to do since those other distracting noises were minimized. Once his confidence levels were established, we resumed playing those background sounds that Blackie too has come to enjoy.

Speaking to him more frequently builds a feeling of security for him, but you must also remember he has two primary senses. You also need to consider how he may be interpreting various scents, even if you can't smell any of them, and help him to make confident choices.

Tips from Blackie's journey: Anxiety at feeding time

Our pack generally eats two meals a day, at the same time each day. When Blackie started his journey, this meant five bowls of dog food all came out at the same time. While some of the other pack members would get excited as soon as they saw the bowls (particularly Jazmine, who has probably the most constant hunger gene I've ever seen in a dog), they were doing so as a result of what they *saw*. Blackie, being unable to see, would guess that it was feeding time but I could still see his anxiety, wondering if it meant that he would be fed. As discussed earlier, one of the effects of blindness can be that their appetite will seem to have increased as they effectively *fear* not knowing when they will next be fed or perhaps, as was the case in our home, get any food while competing with other members of the pack.

I found that talking to Blackie about preparing his meal helped to calm his anxiety and often to simultaneously instill excitement in him, similar to that of the rest of the pack when they saw the bowls approaching. As soon as we would start setting the bowls down, however, Blackie was instantly confused. He would hear the other dogs eating and smell the foods around him, rather than staying focused solely on the bowl in front of him, which he could not see.

Eventually we realized that it was necessary to separate the area where Blackie ate his food, so as to not be too near the other dogs, minimizing their distracting eating noises. Giving Blackie his bowl of food first also brought a sigh of relief that he was indeed being fed, albeit to the dismay of the rest of the pack who could watch Blackie seemingly being the first priority at feeding time (which he was). Over a short period of time, this became habit and has continued to maintain Blackie's confidence at feeding time.

These types of minor modifications will also help maintain his dignity—just because he's blind, doesn't mean he's the last in the pack or family to be fed. Even if you don't have a pack that competes at feeding time with your blind dog, focusing on talking to him and recognizing how other sounds and scents around him may affect his anxiety level are important to building his confidence.

Touching

The focus on monitoring and minimizing his anxiety level needs to extend beyond feeding time and the buffet of scents that will come across his nose, and should include touching. This is not to suggest that his sense of touch becomes a primary sense, but rather to emphasize the importance of you using your touch to create more total trust. Touching your blind dog in a way that reinforces good behavior or good manners has both an immediate calming effect as well as being an overall contributor to building his confidence. Elevate the energy he feels in your touch at every possible interaction, particularly early in his journey. But remember to talk to him before touching him, so that you don't startle him.

A human example would be when you receive praise from a loved one. What gives you the most satisfying feeling: words of praise, a pat on the back with those words, or a big hug with those words? The answer is, of course, the big hug. This ties in nicely with how your blind dog sees through his heart. The next time you give him praise and want to pat him on the head, instead invest an extra few seconds to squat or kneel down, praise him, and touch him in a loving way, such as a non-threatening hug or, even better, long, full body strokes.

Tips from Blackie's journey: The two-handed head-to-head squeeze

Prior to becoming blind, Blackie was never much of a hugger. We knew that, and were appropriately cautious when trying to use extended touch as a means to build his confidence. What I learned through trial and error was that the most effective way to use touch as a reward and calming tool was to squat, kneel, or lean down so that my head was at the same level as his, face to face, and affectionately squeeze the sides of his face below his ears, with a little scratching added in, while praising him at the same time.

This particular example with Blackie is actually a much more insightful illustration of how to connect with your blind dog physically and psychologically. Yes, the use of my touch while praising is a strong connector, but by bringing my face down near his while talking, he can simultaneously hear my voice up close without looking up and also take comfort in smelling me easily. Touch, hearing, and smell all work together to provide a sense of security, while the words themselves express praise.

You should test some variations of this example by observing how much more receptive your blind dog is when you speak to him at that head-to-head level where he doesn't need to look up toward you while decoding the sound or tone of your voice. Think about your own life experiences. If your boss came to your desk and talked to you from a standing position while you were seated, the physicality of her looking down at you would sometimes be intimidating. Equally, if you went to your boss's office and stood in front of her desk while she was seated, the conversation would likely still be intimidating for you. This is because you inherently understand the hierarchy of the boss and employee relationship. Now consider how different the conversation would feel if you and your boss met and talked while both of you were standing up. Most of the time, it would feel like a normal or collaborative conversation. It's a much better feeling.

Your dog inherently thinks of you as the "alpha dog," the highest-ranking member of the household. This is not too dissimilar to the boss and employee relationship that you have likely experienced. By squatting, kneeling, or leaning down to his level, even though he cannot see you, his senses of hearing and smell combine to tell him it's you and at that instant, you will be able to connect without any superior and subordinate context. Don't worry, you won't lose your status as the alpha dog, but you will observe the calming and bonding effect this will have.

No hitting, and scolding must be rare

Firstly, I have rarely ever hit any of my dogs except in a teaching moment when they potentially put their own life at risk, and even then, only gently. These rare occurrences have been limited to going into the street without me or my permission, and when they attempt to eat something outside of our home that is unknown to me and could therefore be dangerous. Fortunately, these incidents have been infrequent as we live in Discovery Bay on Lantau Island in Hong

Kong, a community that doesn't allow personal cars, only golf carts and public buses[7].

Secondly, you can *never* hit a blind dog! It borders on insanity and cruelty, while breaking any sense of total trust that you want and need to have with your companion.

But your blind dog, like all dogs, is at some point going to do something stupid for which you will want and need to reprimand them. You can't hit them, and you need to learn to avoid scolding as much as possible, with one exception being the "no no no" command we'll discuss later in the section on old and new commands. When your blind dog needs a reprimand or correction, you need to turn it into a

---

[7] The restrictions on vehicles in Discovery Bay are not a matter of affluence but of practicality, as it's a small community that until 2000 was only accessible by ferry. Nevertheless, the absence of many vehicles makes it truly one of the most dog-friendly places on earth, particularly given the safety associated with walking your dog without a leash but still under your control. For these reasons, many dog owners like myself take pride in adopting or fostering multiple rescue dogs into their homes. The Discovery Bay community is believed to have more dogs than households.

teaching moment that allows him to realize with confidence that he will not be punished if he does something wrong inadvertently.

Tips from Blackie's journey: No biting

Blackie was not an aggressive dog before losing his sight, but in those early days of darkness he would occasionally make a biting motion toward others in the pack or a human that touched him unexpectedly. This was particularly the case around feeding time, and can still flare up when he encounters a strange dog that gets too close to him on a walk if the socializing time is poorly managed.

When the flare-ups occurred, rather than scold Blackie—we never say, "Bad Boy, Blackie"—I would talk to him as I gently separated him from the proximity of the flare-up, and then sit down with him while touching and continuing to talk to him in a calm manner. He knows when he hasn't been a good boy but his reaction is the result of blindness anxiety causing him to be defensive. I know he didn't understand all of the words I was saying, but the reassurance created by not hitting or scolding him, but rather using a reassuring tone and trying to comfort him from what he perceived as a dangerous situation was fully understood.

I haven't seen Blackie make any type of biting motion in at least two years now. Instead, he learned through his own process that there was no need to attack a potential offender, but that it was useful to warn them that he didn't like what was happening by merely whipping his head quickly in the direction of the potential offender so that he gets his peaceful warning message across.

Working with your blind dog to erase these types of unwanted reactions or behaviors is easy when you remember the importance of building his confidence that he's in a safe environment and using a reassuring tone of voice. Total trust.

Routines create foundations that are safe

Routines establish the security of expectations. Your blind dog needs routines. He takes comfort in knowing what to expect.

The five most basic daily activities are feeding, drinking, going potty, sleeping, and resting (or just hanging out). The principal concept of routines should include when, where, and how.

1.   <u>Feeding</u> – Feeding times should be routine in terms of approximate time of day, just as they are with sighted dogs. Consider where the feeding takes place to ensure it's in a seemingly safe part of your home, hopefully positioned so that he will not be distracted by other sounds. You need to use the same location every day, preferably one that's easy for him to go to instinctively from where he normally hangs out. We made sure that Blackie's feeding location is at least two body lengths away from his water bowl. The process of feeding him (the "how") involves using the same bowl for every meal. As a result of having a pack at our house, we save one specific bowl just for feeding Blackie.

Tips from Blackie's journey: Feeding bowl location

We realized that Blackie repositions his body often while eating, usually because of sounds he hears and his attempts to figure out what they are. If we placed his feeding bowl too close to his water bowl, we might as well plan on getting out the mop to clean up the water he spills as he accidentally knocks into the water bowl while eating. By keeping his feeding location two body lengths away, we're able to prevent the accidental water spills while still letting him know that the water is nearby, as he will often take a drink after eating.

2.   <u>Drinking</u> – I've already discussed several water bowl observations. We keep his water bowl ready for him at all times.

Tips from Blackie's journey: Time to drink

Blackie often goes an extended period of time without getting up to drink. This isn't unusual given a little bit of anxiety associated with moving around. He has never completely learned the command to "drink," but I observed that if he hears fresh water being put into the water bowl, he will usually get up to drink. Similarly, if he happens to be walking or standing near his water, reaching down and tapping on the bowl, encouraging him to drink, also frequently works well. The key here is to identify a command or sound that is a good acoustic way to use his sense of hearing to prompt him to drink.

3.   Going potty – Letting your blind dog go potty is not much different than with a sighted dog; make it routine in terms of times of day (e.g., morning, after meals, etc.). The "where" and "how" he goes are intertwined, as you want to ensure it's a location that's easily accessed and navigated to for him to feel safe and anxiety-free while doing his doody.

Tips from Blackie's journey: Doody time

Blackie is able to urinate and go doody freely in our yard, which provides a convenient and easily accessed location. However, as he exits into the yard, there's a step down to the grass area which, in the early days of his blindness, he always forgot about. We would help remind him by accompanying him past the step to the grass before releasing him. He soon started to remember and "map" that the step was there (this concept is discussed later in the section on simplifying your home). Equally important was remaining there to remind him about the step when he was ready to return indoors.

Another observation was that many times as he finishes urinating, he inadvertently steps in the urine as he puts his lifted leg back to the ground. This also frequently happens on walks when he stops to urinate. This isn't correctable (for male blind dogs), as balancing himself on three legs while urinating creates a little anxiety, and since he cannot see where the urine may have gone, it will always be an occasional occurrence. As such, we've learned to use a doggie wipe to clean his paws regularly when he returns into the house.

4. <u>Sleeping</u> – Many dogs have a favorite place to sleep and perhaps bedding to sleep on. You should make sure that the location is in close proximity to his water bowl in case he's thirsty during the night.

Tips from Blackie's journey: Bells in the night

Early in his journey, when we were using the bell on Blackie's collar to monitor his movements, we found it very helpful during the night to observe his activities. It was clear that he had some level of anxiety when he would awaken, unsure where he was. I could only imagine the pain of waking up and realizing every day is still dark. We would offer him words of support whenever this occurred, observing how the sound of our voice helped alleviate his anxiety. Eventually he was able to sleep well and has accepted the reality of his blindness. My warrior, he is such an inspiration.

5.   Hanging out / resting – Some dogs have a different place in the house just to hang out or chill during the day. The same principles apply to ensure that location is clutter-free and allows easy access for him to perhaps get to and from his water bowl when left alone. You should also consider how sounds in any

particular location may affect your blind dog when you're away.

Tips from Blackie's journey: Favorite chill spots

Blackie seems to have three spots in the house that he hangs out at, depending on his mood or perhaps room temperatures: a tiled area with cool flooring, an area with a rug that isn't as cool as the tiled flooring, and a hidden area in another room. We observed that when it rained outside, he would prefer to go into that other room where the sounds of rain and thunder can't be heard as loudly.

Halo harness

I can't finish a discussion on building confidence in your blind dog without discussing our use of a halo harness[8]. In short, we equipped Blackie with a halo harness and found it to be the most effective

---

[8] Halo harnesses for blind dogs can be found online through websites including Muffin's Halo (muffinshalo.com), which includes the story of Muffin, a poodle who went blind due to cataracts. They're also available from larger retailers, including amazon.com.

accessory to build his confidence while outside of the home. A halo harness is an innovative guide device with a lightweight tube that serves as a bumper, extending around the dog's head and helping to protect it when he bumps into things. It is an ingenious aid to help a blind dog become familiar with new areas and surroundings by learning to change direction while safely avoiding injury.

Due to the size of the halo and the smaller areas within our home, it wasn't very effective indoors. However, I found it to be the major confidence builder for him when he went outside the home and yard. For this reason, it's only mentioned briefly here and discussed further in the chapter on simplifying your walks later herein.

7 SIMPLIFY YOUR HOME

Maps + music + lemon juice + vanilla + guards = a happy home

Try this exercise:

1. Read and memorize this list.
2. Find a blindfold.
3. Go lay in your bed and put the blindfold on.
4. Keep your vision completely covered as you do the rest of these steps.
5. Get out of bed and go to your bathroom.

6. Leave the bathroom and go to your microwave oven.
7. Next go to your refrigerator.
8. Now go sit on your couch.
9. Get off your couch and return to your bed.
10. Lay there for a minute. You're done.

Now go do it before you continue reading.

* * * * * * * * *

How did it go? I would be surprised if you didn't bump into things or even fall down along the way. Welcome to the world of sudden blindness, even in your home. Your blind dog has faced the same challenge of trying to navigate between where he sleeps, rests, eats, drinks, and goes potty. In order to remember where these important locations are, he "maps" in his mind how to get around to each of them—I introduced the concept of mapping briefly in Chapter 2, Understanding blindness, as the combined effect of a blind dog using their senses of hearing and smelling for mapping in his mind where they are and where they want to go. A blind dog uses its memory of a general area, the sounds associated with that area and the various scents that may vary every step or few steps. As his seeing eye human, you have to both help him learn which maps are important, and periodically update his maps as necessary.

The primary location for mapping is your home, in which your blind dog spends the majority of his days and all of his nights. Mapping of the areas he visits frequently for walks or playtime are also important, and discussed later. As general guidance, I found that repeated daily exposure to different areas of the house over five to seven days allowed Blackie to sufficiently map his home ... until we changed something. This then required another five to seven days for him to re-map it.

Let's discuss what you can do to make him comfortable and feel safe in his home.

Mapping

Time for another exercise. In our earlier exercise, you had to simulate blindness and how you would navigate from bed to go potty, to eat, to drink, to rest, and then go back to bed. Before you can help your blind dog with his mapping, you need to see and hear what he does. So now try this.

Get on your knees, preferably without a television or music playing. Start at his sleeping location, and now spend a few minutes crawling around, calling upon your superpower of observation. What is in the way of you getting from place to place? Is there a table at dog height with a sharp-cornered edge? What are the textures of your furniture that he will inevitably bump into (e.g., a couch is likely soft and long, whereas a table leg is hard and narrow)? Are there kitchen chairs in the way? What can you see that may have a strong smell (e.g., a pair of dirty, smelly slippers)? Where are the steps or stairs? Do you have hardwood floors, tiles, carpets, or rugs? Are the floors completely flat? Do doors have thresholds from one room to another?

Pause along the way and observe by listening, Are there any sounds (e.g., children playing outside, a neighbor's footsteps, etc.)?

How was it? What are the things that may affect your blind dog's ability to get around comfortably and safely? Now ask each of the other members of your household to do the same and compare notes. You should now be able to prepare a list of the things to consider modifying to help your blind dog map his home more easily.

You aren't likely to relocate furniture, as there's no need to do so. You may move a few things to make an area less cluttered, but your blind dog will learn his way around. And after about five to seven days of making sure everything stays the same, he should be able to adequately map the home. During this first week and thereafter, continue to use your superpower of observation to see if there are any objects that he repeatedly bumps into or struggles to pass by, and consider what you can do to ease his path.

Tips from Blackie's journey: Who put that there?

Long after Blackie had mapped his primary living area, stretching between the living and dining rooms, we decided to move the bed of another one of our dogs to a cooler area. We had forgotten to consider what this would mean for Blackie, as it was close to his hanging out area and directly in a path to the chair on which I usually sit. As a result, he would repeatedly walk into that dog bed, which was only a couple inches high, and he would then freeze. He was confused, wondering what had changed. After observing it twice, we knew we had to help him learn to re-map that path, rather than move the dog bed. Just like the first time, after about five to seven days his mapping "update" was successfully downloaded.

Mapping is your blind dog's way of knowing his world of darkness. If someone moves something, or places something in his mapped paths, he will try to update his maps. His maps are only effective as long as his mapped routes don't change.

Sounds

The best thing you can do is to merely recognize the sounds your blind dog regularly hears in his home, and those other sounds (usually from the outside) that cause him to trigger either into a frozen or alert state. His heightened hearing will pick up every noise, including some that you won't even hear. An example could be an analog wall clock with a faint ticking sound; eventually he will map where that is. Louder sounds and those that are not always present, such as children playing or adults talking, are the ones that will be most likely to cause a reaction. We have found that having a television or music as a low-level background noise continuously during the day helps to mask the other sounds he hears, putting him at peace with confidence.

Outside sounds are the ones we can't predict or control. Blackie often hears people talking as they pass by our house that we do not hear, and only recognize when we open the door and look out. With human passersby, he gets alerted and listens, whereas when another dog passes by outside, he will often jump up and head toward the door. We keep the path between his usual spots to the doorway clear so that he doesn't trip over something.

> *Tips from Blackie's journey: The sound of silence*
>
> At bedtime, our television and music are shut off most nights. However, when there's rain forecasted overnight, we'll leave some sound playing at a much lower level just to help soothe the effect of those unexpected noises that may startle him from the sound of silence, which can be broken quickly by rainfall or thunder.

Smells and scenting

With sounds you can wait and recognize what your blind dog hears, but you just can't appreciate all of the smells and scents that he picks up on given the difference between his sense of smell and yours. The exceptions are when your home is filled with cooking smells, or that pair of dirty, smelly slippers left in the living room.

However, you can still use scents as a mapping aid as illustrated below.

Tips from Blackie's journey: Lemon juice drops

After noticing that Blackie would hesitate as he moved from one room to another or attempted to go outside the patio door (which involved a rather awkward step), we started placing a few drops of lemon juice in these doorways. Lemon juice drops are harmless but have a strong scent (at least to dogs) and gave Blackie confidence to know when he was approaching a doorway. Once he'd comfortably mapped these locations, we discontinued scenting the doorways on a regular basis, but still do so periodically as a friendly reminder.

Think about what areas of your blind dog's home may benefit from scenting to help with his mapping. Don't forget to periodically reapply the same scents to the same locations.

Stairs

I haven't discussed stairs yet as it's important to first accomplish the basics of mapping and remembering the importance of his primary senses, hearing and smell. My house has two levels of stairs so we learned very quickly that we had to teach Blackie how to get up and down them. Generally speaking, going up stairs does not create much anxiety while going down any stairs is filled with cautious apprehension, even several years later.

In the next chapter I discuss how to use commands, including for going up and down the stairs. For now, I want to continue the discussion on scenting through another example with Blackie.

Tips from Blackie's journey: Vanilla not chocolate steps

I observed that Blackie's cautious apprehension about stairs could often be noticed when he was six feet away from them (a rather long distance) and even if going up or down the stairs wasn't planned. I decided that scenting the top and bottom of each staircase could be worthwhile and decided to use vanilla extract, yet another harmless but distinct scent that he can associate solely with the staircases. You probably already know that you can never use chocolate, as it is fatally harmful to dogs.

I actually had a small issue to overcome as our floors and staircases are not carpeted. If we placed the drops of vanilla extract on the flooring, they would be cleaned away daily and a hectic household with a pack would likely make it difficult to remember to re-scent the staircases every day. I found a practical solution by cutting a small unused rug into little strips that could be scented with the vanilla extract and placed at each of these locations. We try to re-scent them about once every ten days, or when we wash the rug strips.

Blackie immediately mapped the stairs with confidence, knowing that he did not need to be threatened by where the stairs may be located, as he could effectively see them through his sense of smell with the vanilla extract.

Guards and bumpers

Hopefully you didn't bump your head when you did the earlier blindfolded exercise; if you did, you have further experienced what will inevitably happen to your blind dog. With any luck, during the second exercise, when you were crawling around at your dog's level, you identified those items in his home that he's more likely than not to bump into, and further branded the dangerous ones. We initially found two items that we had to install some bumper guards on so that he wouldn't hurt himself.

Tips from Blackie's journey: Bumper cars are fun; bumper dogs are not

The furniture in our house is generally harmless if a dog bumps into it, but we do have a coffee table and end table that are lower in height with cornered edges. We purchased rubber bumper guards to put on all of the cornered edges that are exposed to Blackie's walking areas so that if he did bump into one, there would be no chance of injury or otherwise that would cause him to have anxiety with his map. I have actually never seen

Blackie bump into any of them, but knowing he's safe around the home in case he did makes me feel more secure.

I also observed that a particular piece of furniture also seemed to make Blackie freeze in his tracks, another sign of anxiety. Specifically, it's a square-shaped wooden bed post that he needs to navigate around to reach a particular set of stairs. I can only deduce that because the wood is a hard surface with corners, it causes anxiety arising with respect to how close he may be to the stairs, despite the drops of vanilla extract on the rug strip about four feet away. Innovation was necessary, so we took a thick bath towel and wrapped it around the bedpost. Success! Total trust restored.

8 OLD AND NEW COMMANDS

You can't teach an old dog new tricks

This adage is fiction not fact when helping a blind dog learn to navigate his world of darkness. The real trick is to not confuse his new commands with his old ones.

The best guidance here is to consider commands that essentially help you to steer your blind dog. And remember the basics about teaching any commands are to keep them short, only one or two syllables (e.g., "sit" or "roll over"). Basic commands can be very helpful, including "left" (to turn or steer left), "right" (to turn or steer right), "straight" (to stop him from turning), and "stop."

I must admit that I was never successful at teaching Blackie to turn left or right. It sometimes worked, but sometimes didn't and I eventually gave up as everything seemed a bit too overwhelming for him. Nevertheless, Blackie successfully learned other commands.

One example is "drink", whereby your blind dog knows he can drink water from a particular spot. Hopefully you'll be more successful than I was with Blackie. We continue to make feeble attempts with the command "drink," although for the most part Blackie has since become self-sufficient in getting enough water, mostly due to the sounds of the water or tapping on the water bowl as described in an earlier tip.

A couple more examples warrant more detail and can best be conveyed by sharing my experiences.

Tips from Blackie's journey: "Step" and "down"

Teaching Blackie that a step was imminent presented the need for a decision about what commands to use. He had previously known the command "up" as an instruction to stand up or to get up on something, so using that as a consistent command for going up stairs seemed logical, and proved to be effective.

Going down the stairs caused a new challenge as he knew the command "down" meant to get down from something or to lie down, and would likely continue to be used in that context. I decided on the command "step" to be used as it was a single word command not likely to be confused with any other commands. It too proved to be effective. We taught him this initially by guiding him with our hands and afterward by loosely holding his lift assist harness (which is discussed later herein), clearly and repeatedly giving the command "step" for each and every step downward. Each successful movement down a step is followed by a "good" or "good boy" to reinforce the proper behavior, and another "step." There are no exceptions. As his seeing eye human, it's my job to ensure he's guided down every step with the command to continue to reinforce his sense of security. Total trust.

This command is also quite useful when we go on our walks and he needs to navigate a curb or uneven surface.

Tips from Blackie's journey: No no no

Almost every dog understands the word "no" and that it distinctly means not to do something, usually because a person sees the dog doing something improper. Blackie was no different. However, using the word "no" around a blind dog will immediately cause confusion for him, because he can't see whether you're speaking to him or another dog or perhaps even a child in your household. Nevertheless, he had it etched in his memory that the word "no" meant that he should not do something or stop doing something.

The additional issue we had was that we wanted to avoid using commands that tend to come across as scolding, which the command "no" certainly has a tendency to do. Human nature means that the word "no" usually comes out with a raised voice and disciplinary tone, and we wanted to avoid the unintended consequence of that causing anxiety, particularly if he couldn't immediately determine if it was being directed at him or to another dog or person.

We decided to develop the command "no no no" that was to be used only for Blackie and not the other pack members, in order for him to stop an action or to stop his forward movement. We only say it in a monotone voice without any tonal emphasis so that it comes across as a safety or—in the case of our walks—corrective command, rather than a disciplinary or otherwise negative command that may cause anxiety. Total trust. The "no no no" command has been hugely successful in instilling that sense of security without the negative connotations that result in him thinking he has misbehaved, thereby assisting with his sense of confidence both inside and outside of the home.

Yes, you can teach an old dog—even an old blind dog—new tricks.

9 SIMPLIFY YOUR WALKS

Who wants to go for a walk?

Your blind dog still needs the activity of walking and this can't stop just because he's blind. However, it's normal that his anxiety level about going outside will be heightened until you simplify your walks and give him the confidence to leave the safety of his home. I couldn't imagine living life without being able to take Blackie on walks.

I found there to be three elements that really opened up Blackie's world to continue to go on walks with

me and made him feel safe and confident: use of a
halo harness (as briefly introduced earlier), developing
safe and fun walking routes, and having multiple
walking routes to vary the routine.

Halo harness

As briefly highlighted earlier, Blackie's halo harness
was the most effective accessory to build his
confidence while outside of the home. As you can see
in the photo, the halo-like tube is fixed to a body
harness to be positioned over his head, and serves as
a lightweight bumper that helps protect his head if he
comes up against any objects while moving around.
The halo harness was the best money we ever spent

to help build Blackie's confidence so that he can once again enjoy going on walks.

While I've read stories of halo harnesses being used on small dogs inside their homes, Blackie's medium size and the smaller areas within our home didn't facilitate indoor use. This probably worked to our benefit, as Blackie started to associate putting on his halo harness with preparing to go on a safe walk with me.

Tips from Blackie's journey: His first steps as an angel

I joked frequently that I had two angels: my other dog named Angel, and Blackie who looked like an angel complete with a halo. When we first put the halo harness on Blackie, he understandably found it cumbersome even though it's actually lightweight; it just took a little getting used to.

As a result, the first few days he had it on, he stood motionless outside our door needing a nudge to start walking. I would stand alongside him to coach him but he would only take baby steps. I decided to attach my leash to his harness to allow me to be ahead of him and coach him with little tugs on the leash. It worked. After probably two to three days, Blackie was totally comfortable wearing his halo harness, and no longer needed me alongside him or on a leash. I could see his confidence strengthening on each walk we took. Success!

I continued to have Blackie wear his halo harness until I felt like he had adequately mapped our walking routes, and his angel-like halo was then retired.

Safe and fun walking routes

In Blackie's case, his new walking routes were merely shorter versions of his old neighborhood walks. Sadly, I had to cut out his beach walks and our hikes. The neighborhood provided a great abundance of grassy areas, trees, bushes, and plenty of scents for him to pick up. It's also free of any fast-moving vehicles, so very safe in that respect.

The safety challenges we did have to face are likely some of the same that you will encounter, such as:

- Trees, bushes, and light posts
- Uneven ground
- Inclined areas
- Differences in grass texture when it's been cut
- Occasional spraying of pesticides
- Snakes (hopefully you don't have this!)
- Unexpected appetizing items
- Other dogs
- People

Having a variety of scents for your blind dog to sniff is incredibly stimulating for him and will help keep him motivated about going on walks. I found and still find myself mustering more patience with him on our walks as he does linger much longer on scents now than when he had vision.

Whereas the mapping of his home took only about five to seven days, largely due to the confined space and limited number of variables, mapping regular routes outdoors will take much longer. However, you will see his confidence building walk by walk, and he should quickly become excited rather than nervous to go on those walks. In Blackie's case, he wore his halo harness for nearly three months before we gradually started reducing the wear and eventually retired it. I no longer saw a need for him to wear it as he'd mapped the majority of our walking routes very well and began to effectively use his sense of smell as a bumper for at least those obstacles with distinct scents.

Tips from Blackie's journey: The root of the problem

One of our routes includes an open grassy area that's often used as a small playing area for the neighborhood dogs. My entire pack had always loved going there and ganging up on whichever pack member was the pick of the day. We had avoided going there on Blackie's initial walks, given the presence of other dogs, but at some point we put it back into our route. Blackie loved it, despite the fact that he couldn't run around like the other dogs. One day, perhaps a year after we had started returning there, I took my eyes off Blackie for a moment and suddenly heard him cry. He never cries. I ran over immediately and it turned out that he had misstepped and tripped over the roots of a tree that were protruding from the ground. He had been there many times, felt it was a safe area and had just been startled when he tripped over one of the roots. There was no lasting injury but my conscience was dented as my momentary lapse in observing him was poorly timed. I have since realized that I must keep my superpower of observation on even in places he and I may have visited many times.

Vary the routine

Once your blind dog has your walking routes mapped out, it's also important to vary them. While you may find the same walking routine to be boring based on seeing the same thing on every walk, remember that your blind dog sees with his nose and the smells he takes in probably make even the routine walks very enjoyable.

Nevertheless, your blind dog will stay stimulated if you vary the routine walks and also take him on other walks too, as he'll thrive on the new scents he picks up on a new route.

Remember too to vary who he walks with, as he will also appreciate the changes in companionship on his walks. This could mean having a different household member walk him or, in our case, deciding which other members of the pack go on our walks with us. I also find it important to take Blackie on some solo walks as he relishes having me all to himself, and I'm usually able to be more attentive to observing him.

Tips from Blackie's journey: Smell the roses

Often when I go on the solo just-him-and-I walks, I'll pick a new place to walk to. I can almost immediately see him realize that it's an area he hasn't mapped out. I resume the old practice of walking alongside him, reassuring him that we are on a safe route. He gradually gets more comfortable and then seems to happily lose himself in the abundance of new and differing scents he picks up. On one such occasion, we wandered to an area with a lot of wildflowers (perhaps not exactly roses) and he was completely intoxicated, picking up on the overwhelming number of scents that were present.

10 PLAYTIME

Who wants to play?

By this time, your blind dog has mapped his must-
know places, has his confidence back, feels safe, and
is really starting to enjoy the brightness of his life— in
large part because of you, his seeing eye human. It's
now time to learn all over again how to play as part of
his new everyday quality of life.

Your blind dog needs playtime, whether it's indoors
or outdoors. It's best when this comes after the basic
foundations are built so that he feels safe to enjoy his

playtime. There's no magical list of what playtime activity your blind dog will enjoy best, just that it should be safe and will inevitably be less active than what a dog with vision can do.

Playtime should initially be structured so that your dog is alone with you, and is the center of your attention. You need to again call on your superpower of observation to be acutely aware of his surroundings when playing to avoid distractions (particularly sounds and other people and dogs) and any obstacles that may be in close proximity, or suddenly present themselves. You need to ensure it's a safe, distraction-free environment so that he can focus on playing.

Experiment. You're likely to find that your blind dog no longer cares for some of the same activities he used to when he could see, and he's very likely to gain interest in new activities, particularly those that engage his primary senses of hearing and smell. Experiment, but continue to be aware of his surroundings.

As for Blackie, he suddenly liked to play catch with a ball as it engaged his primary senses: listen for the ball coming through the air, bouncing, and then let the sniffer kick in to smell it out. Mind you, I wasn't throwing the ball far, rarely more than about five feet, but he relished it. Interestingly, before going blind he had little interest in ever playing catch or fetch, but now he loved playing "ball." Sadly, Blackie had a very serious head trauma accident when he vigorously chased a ball that he deflected in another direction and he ran into a light post. I do not dwell on that here, but I do describe the resulting alternate journey we traveled in Appendix B: Blackie's history. Suffice it to say that whatever your playtime activity, expect the unexpected. Even since his accident, Blackie still relishes his playtime, albeit that there is no more playing ball.

Tips from Blackie's journey: He likes to watch

One of Blackie's favorite playtime activities is hanging out with the pack when they're chasing each other. He just stands there and seemingly watches them play. At first, I thought it appeared quite sad because he couldn't participate like the others. However, I came to appreciate that he was, in fact, watching them with his primary senses of hearing and smell. I suspect that somewhere in his mind he has tucked away memories of when he took part in these activities, and it helps him to enjoy what he hears and smells. His mood always seems to be very upbeat and energized when he does this.

11 ACCESSORIZING HELPS

What does that collar say?

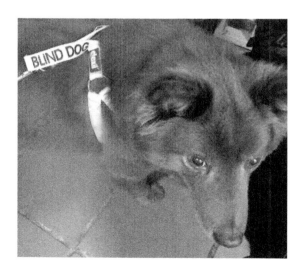

Earlier I described the halo harness as an accessory. While this is true, I wasn't intending it to be compared to how you might accessorize an outfit to enhance its aesthetic appeal. Your blind dog will care less about how he looks and he certainly won't be able to see himself in a mirror.

The concept of accessorizing for a blind dog is all about confidence, or security and safety. The halo harness was, in my experience, the single best accessory for instilling confidence in Blackie and giving him a sense of security while walking outdoors.

Another useful accessory I've already mentioned is a small bell on his collar that makes a sound to alert you to his movements during the day or night. This falls in the security and safety category, as you can observe him to see if he needs anything.

There are two other accessories I've found to be useful in the security and safety category: blind dog alert collars and anxiety jackets.

Blind dog alert collars

It's funny how most dog lovers get excited about a new collar for their companion. We're no different. In our house, we buy new collars in different colors every Christmas for each of our dogs, and donate their old ones to a dog rescue organization (such as HKDR). Ironically, most dogs dislike wearing a collar but get used to them, regardless of color. But when people come up to a dog, one of the first things they notice is the dog's collar.

This is where the use of a collar that clearly announces your dog is a "BLIND DOG" is very useful, as it puts the approaching person (who may not be known to or remembered by your blind dog) on alert. Your blind dog can't see the person approaching, and if the person's voice and scent aren't recognized, it may result in your blind dog becoming anxious and, in some cases, reacting defensively. Accessorizing your blind dog with an alert collar is a useful way to keep him safe from those people he is less familiar with.

Tips from Blackie's journey: Multiple accessories

I've used a blind dog alert collar almost from day one of discovering Blackie was blind. We have so many other dog owners in our neighborhood and those meeting Blackie for the first time have almost always commented, "oh, is he blind?" Not only does it engage that person's sensitivity to approaching a blind dog, it's a great reminder for me to ask them to be cautious around him as "he cannot see you." Furthermore, since many of these people are accompanied by their own dog, I can also ask them to try to keep their dog at a little distance from Blackie because "he sometimes becomes anxious around other dogs." Once Blackie becomes familiar with the scent of another dog, this is no longer a concern.

The leash that I occasionally use is similarly an alert leash that boldly announces that he is a "BLIND DOG."

After Blackie had his head trauma incident, he started to frequently wear a lift assist harness[9],

---

[9] Blackie's lift assist harness is a Help'em Up® harness. For more information see helpemup.com. Other lift assist harnesses, also called lifting aid harnesses, can be found online through

which is basically a loose-fitting harness with handles on top of his shoulders and rear end that I can grab and lift to assist him in getting to wherever he's going. I've found this particularly useful for him going up and down stairs, as by me merely tugging on one of the handles he feels a sense of security that I'm there to guide him. However, I wouldn't describe this as a necessary accessory for blind dogs in general. Blackie's accident had resulted in a bruised spine, so he had initially needed it for us to merely assist him with standing up. Nevertheless, he continues to wear it often and I have accessorized his lift assist harness with a "BLIND DOG" alert near his shoulders and head area, which also works effectively in alerting people he meets for the first time that he's blind.

Anxiety jackets

An anxiety jacket is a tight-fitting, shirt-like article that embraces a dog's body and provides a calming effect

---

websites including mypetneedsthat.com, which includes a 2020 review of various lift assist harnesses, and Amazon.com.

to offset any anxiety they may be feeling[10]. It should really be called an anti-anxiety jacket. An anxiety jacket isn't intended to be worn all of the time but rather used when something triggers anxiety. They are most commonly used on dogs with full vision when there's a thunderstorm or other large repetitive noises (e.g., nearby construction).

I encourage you to purchase an anxiety jacket for your blind dog, as it's one of those things that you will wish you had immediately when you realize it's needed, so better to have it at the ready. In Blackie's case, he's benefited from wearing it on multiple occasions during typhoon season in Hong Kong. Typhoons are usually not accompanied by thunder but the sounds of strong winds and heavy rains also cause him to have some anxiety.

---

[10] Blackie's anxiety jacket is a ThunderShirt®. For more information see thundershirt.com. Other anxiety jackets can be found online through websites including amazon.com. BestReviews.Guide has a 2020 review of various anxiety jackets at bestreviews.guide/dog-anxiety-jackets.

12 SOCIALIZING

Making friends

Just imagine how you would feel if you had lost your sense of sight and suddenly your family and friends stopped coming to visit you, and never invited you to get together for a dinner date. While the social life of a dog is clearly different, dogs need opportunities to socialize just as much as us humans do.

Socializing with people and other dogs inside and outside their home is essential. With a sighted and healthy dog, these are opportunities for them to have some fun but it also exposes them to a variety of sights, sounds, and smells. The result is usually a happier dog, and a dog that's less reactive in general terms when exposed to other people and dogs in the future.

With your blind dog, the sense of satisfaction he derives from social interactions may not initially be apparent. You need to imagine the times that will come a short way down the road, perhaps weeks but months at most, when he's over the initial apprehensions of encountering other people and dogs. By helping ensure he has these opportunities to socialize, particularly early in the period when he's adapting to his new life of darkness, you're helping him walk as close as possible to the quality of life any other dog can have. We know his life will never fully be his previous "normal," but his new "normal" must include socializing.

I've deliberately separated the modifiers of playtime and socializing, although there is clearly some cross over. The primary reasons for this are that playtime can often be alone with your blind dog, and means a heightened need to limit the extent of activity and be acutely aware of his surroundings. Socializing, on the other hand, often occurs unexpectedly as and when you and he come across an old friend of his and their human.

How dogs socialize

Sighted dogs tend to initiate socializing when they see another dog or person, or perhaps first they hear the other dog or person and they then visually investigate where that sound is coming from. The first contact for sighted dogs when socializing is almost entirely visual, as they interpret body language or visual signals (e.g., another dog owner throwing a stick for his dog to fetch) as the first sign that socializing is about to occur.

This initial sight-trigger may be different if the dog recognizes the other dog or person, assuming you believe—as I do—that dogs with sight do recognize how different people look (Princess can often easily pick me out among a hundred people at our nearby beach area when she wanders off and then turns around to check on me). After recognizing their friend (whether dog or human), and assuming they do not immediately start to participate in an activity such as trying to retrieve that thrown stick first, dogs approach others and immediately begin to smell them. As discussed earlier, this is the primary sense dogs use to remember just about everything. Sure, they may have visually recognized that other human, but it's not until they get up close and either obviously or inconspicuously sniff them that they verify that it is indeed who they thought it was. And we've all seen the not-so-inconspicuous manner in which dogs reacquaint themselves with other dogs by sniffing each other's rear ends.

A blind dog can't take an initial cue through a visual sign. And while blind dogs initially trigger to other humans and dogs by sound, you'll witness your blind dog attempting to figure out who the sound is – friend or new friend or foe. Sadly, many (but not all) blind dogs absorb such sounds in simple terms by assuming it must be a foe, and their defensive or insecure nature becomes apparent. This will slowly subside, and hopefully disappear entirely as I have seen with some blind dogs, as you engage them regularly in socializing.

If the sound of that approaching human is within your house, your blind dog will likely learn and recognize his or her voice quite quickly. This is largely because he assumes you wouldn't let any foe come into your house, and the ambient background sounds competing with the voice of that human are controlled by you or under your control. The at-home environment makes for a much more comfortable "meet and greet" when socializing with other humans.

This isn't the case with other dogs given that dogs don't speak so there is no voice for your blind dog to learn or recognize. If your friend comes over with their dog, you'll see your blind dog initially be very alert and alarmed, possibly barking at the approaching dog even if he has played with them hundreds of times. Take your time in getting them reacquainted.

When encounters occur outside your house, even with humans that your blind dog has known for years, that cautious and guarded apprehension will be there for some time even if he recognizes the other human's voice. This is a reflection of the less controlled environment outside, which naturally puts your blind dog on a higher state of alert and is likely filled with many sounds that may not be so obvious to you (remember, his hearing is so much more acute than yours). Thus, your superpower of observation needs to be fully switched on as those initial parts of the socializing start to occur.

Eventually your blind dog will move onto their most important sense when socializing: smelling the visiting human or dog to see if it's a friend they remember, or setting the stage to be a new friend. You should only allow this "meet and sniff" in a fully controlled setting. Keep your superpower on, in case you need to intervene to avoid an undesirable incident. You need to reassure your blind dog that this is a friend, perhaps through what you say and the tone of your voice. And you must expect that every encounter is going to result in the inevitable attempted rear-end sniff, usually by the other dog first particularly if the other dog has the ability to see. If the other dog moves too quickly, it will startle your blind dog.

Tips from Blackie's journey: Let me help you smell her

I like to help Blackie with those first sniffs that are about to happen. But no, I don't get down on my knees and try to sniff around the other dog's rear end.

I've found that continuously talking to Blackie to provide reassurance that the approaching dog or human is our friend is helpful. With the other person, I ask them to put the back of their hand out and let Blackie smell it. This works quite well. With other dogs, I try to reach over to the other dog, while maintaining appropriate separation between Blackie and the other dog, and pet them while letting Blackie hear that I am doing so, sometimes with a "good boy / girl" thrown in for good measure. I then let Blackie smell the hand that I petted the other dog with to have an initial scent of who it is.

If he's still on a guarded alert, then the rear-end sniff is just not going to be allowed. But most of the time this initial scent eases Blackie into an accepting mood and we're able to let the two dogs "get to know each other".

This exposure to socializing tends to invigorate their primary senses of hearing and smell. And the more you let them socialize by exposing them to other people and other dogs, the more you'll see it is a happy time for them and the stronger their overall confident feeling of security will continue to be.

Tips from Blackie's journey: A little too excitable

My current oldest dog, Jazmine, is a Chocolate Labrador Retriever. She's also known as "Granny J" since she's approaching her 14th birthday, which is nearly 100 in dog years. Jazmine is about the friendliest big dog in the world and in her earlier years served as a "Dr Dog," a therapy dog who would frequently visit local hospitals, nursing homes, and children's centers in Hong Kong to spread her amazing ability to make people smile while cultivating among these people a good impression about what a loving companion a dog can be[11]. A few years ago, a neighbor was so smitten by Jazmine that she adopted a Chocolate Labrador Retriever puppy herself, whom she named Rasmus. Rasmus was full of tremendous energy as a pup and would always get the members of my pack worked up when we would encounter him on a neighborhood walk. As an adult, Rasmus continues to have these energy boosts every time we see him.

Blackie, who's about eight years older than Rasmus, had known and played with Rasmus many times before he lost his sight. When we first reintroduced our blind Blackie to Rasmus, we were cautious and slow, and these two old friends seem to have an occasional "bromance". Admittedly, this gave myself and Rasmus's human a false sense of comfort. One day when they were socializing, and I was not exercising my superpower, we heard Blackie make the sound of a potential biting growl. We turned just in time to see Rasmus, who had obviously had a burst of his puppy-like energy, turn and move rapidly away

---

[11] For more information go to animalsasia-Dr dog.

from Blackie. No one was hurt, but Blackie clearly didn't appreciate Rasmus's exuberant liveliness, which may sit well with a dog that can see, but not Blackie.

This was a good lesson for me to remember that even when Blackie is among his friends, no one can predict reliably how either dog may provoke the other. As a seeing eye human, your superpower of observation must always be switched on, even when your blind dog has known the other dog for many years and played with them many times before he went blind.

Tackle socializing with your blind dog as early as you can when they begin to get more comfortable inside and outside the house, and construct those building blocks that will allow him to be as great a socializer as he once was—albeit with the obvious limitations that come with his blindness.

Other household dogs

A brief discussion about socializing with other dogs in the same household is worthwhile. I shared earlier

how when Blackie initially suffered his blindness—
that six-week period in which it was not diagnosed
and therefore misunderstood—his behavior around
the rest of the pack had seemingly become aggressive,
but this was actually the defensive nature of a
misunderstood blind dog. This applies equally
whether you have two dogs in your household, a pack
like in mine, or if your household also includes cats.

Blind dogs cherish having another four-legged
companion in their household, even if they can't see
them. Don't let the presence of other pets, currently
or in the future, be a concern for you, other than by
recognizing that you need to help your blind dog re-
learn how to socialize with them. You will also need
to coach your other pets to interact more cautiously
with your blind dog. They're pretty smart, and will get
the hang of it rather quickly. At the same time, be
aware that their natural animal instinct may be to
consider your blind dog as the weakest member of
the pack, but by ensuring that the others don't let this
result in a negative behavior change, they'll all

continue to live in peace (perhaps even more peacefully than before your dog became blind).

Other dogs in the household often act as a companion to a blind dog and may be of great benefit, literally becoming the dog's own "seeing eye dog".

Tips from Blackie's journey: Blackie's big sister

My Granny J, Jazmine, has such a loving personality and she touches the heart of everyone she meets. Given Jazmine's elderly age, she now moves at about the same slower speed that is perfect for accompanying Blackie on his walks (particularly since I don't use a leash for either of them). Jazmine has, in effect, become Blackie's "seeing eye dog" on those walks, as Blackie seems to primarily lock onto the sound of Jazmine's footsteps, and not necessarily mine. I believe it gives Blackie a sense of independence in figuring out where to go without total reliance on me, which is a great feeling for all three of us.

Likewise, Jazmine understands this and frequently pauses, waiting for Blackie to keep up. When Jazmine does pause, and Blackie can no longer hear Jazmine's guiding footsteps, I see Blackie sniffing the air to figure out exactly where Jazmine is and then quickly continuing toward his walking companion.

If you or your household are considering adding another four-legged companion into your house, do not let the presence of your blind dog be a deterrent. He can always use another companion and your chance to give another dog a great life will be a win-win situation for the world of dogs. Hopefully part of your consideration will include adopting a rescue dog and effectively saving a life. The added benefit of a rescue dog, in most cities, is that you may be able to foster the rescue dog for a few weeks to assess how the two of them will get along (but note that even two weeks of fostering may not be enough for a sufficient assessment). The only added challenge to be aware of with a rescue dog is that you cannot fully appreciate the demons that may exist in his or her past that affect the way they socialize with other dogs, let alone a blind dog. This, again, should not be a deterrent; setting the right environment within your house is the only cure that is needed.

* * * * * * * * *

I started this chapter on the magical modifier of socializing by asking you to imagine if suddenly your family and friends stopped coming to visit you. I ask you to now think about how invigorated you feel after a get-together with family or friends. Your blind dog will mirror those feelings of enjoyment and friendship when you enable him to socialize, and to do so frequently.

13 AGING

Aging gracefully? Dogs don't care!

Another great thing about dogs is that they don't have a narcissistic bone in their body. They couldn't care less if some of their hair starts to get gray, unlike us humans. Aging is inevitable and unavoidable.

An aging blind dog is not much different than a sighted dog. They tend to periodically get grumpy (much like aging humans) and become more lethargic, looking to sleep around the house even more than a younger dog.

However, there are a couple of differences to keep in mind with respect to an aging blind dog. Blind dogs generally require a little more focus on nutrition and exercise in comparison to dogs that still have their vision.

Most seasoned dog owners understand the three stages of a dog's life[12] when it comes to feeding them: puppy, adult, and senior. Dog food companies cater quite well to this with a broad selection of flavors and types of food (e.g., wet or dry) for your dog at any stage of his life. I'll leave dog food selection to you, perhaps in consultation with your dog's vet, as this isn't intended to be a text book on canine nutrition.

Nevertheless, with your blind dog, you need to consider that he's almost certainly getting less activity and exercise than he would if he was a fully sighted dog. As a result, his metabolism and overall physical development don't benefit in the same way as most

---

[12] For more information on the nutritional requirements for all stages of a dog's life see Royal Canin's website (https://www.royalcanin.com/au/dogs/nutrition-for-life).

other dogs of a similar age. We tend to have at least an annual discussion with Blackie's vet about his exercise level and any noticeable physical changes we may be observing, particularly when he's standing up from a lying position, going on a walk, going up steps, etc. In fact, we've had these annual discussions throughout his life and not just since he became blind.

Blackie's annual checkup includes blood tests so that we can monitor and evaluate how his organs may be changing. This has resulted in a few variations in dog food over the years, tailored to his changing needs for food high in carbohydrates or protein or a few other components. As I've said, this isn't much different than it would be with a sighted dog, but requires a heightened awareness level with proactive follow-up.

Another proactive step you can take right away is to consider whether your blind dog would benefit from any specific supplements. While this should again be a decision you make yourself, I will share with you that we've been giving Blackie a longevity supplement called Resvantage Canine®,[13] the principal ingredient of which is resveratrol. This supplement has diverse health benefits designed to help support a dog's overall wellness, including healthy joint function and digestive and neurological support, and is safe for long-term daily use. All dogs are different, and selecting the best supplement or supplements to compensate for your blind dog's reduced activity and exercise levels should be specific to their individual case, perhaps in consultation with their vet.

Please remember that this is not a textbook on canine nutrition, but rather a discussion of the modifiers associated with aging that I think will help you keep your blind dog's nutrition at the forefront, given his relatively lower levels of exercise compared with those of sighted dogs. His aging is inevitable, but you can help him avoid nutritional deficiencies that may unexpectedly arise as a result of his lifestyle as a blind dog.

---

[13] Resvantage Canine® is available from a number of retailers, including amazon.com.

Tips from Blackie's journey: Meal choices

Our friend who originally adopted Blackie is a vegan. As a result, we've always had a propensity to consider a mix of cooked vegetables as part of the food that Blackie eats, as well as the rest of our pack. This has thus far worked well in a general context as he's been content with the mix that we've provided him with.

Recently we've noticed that chewing dry food is starting to become a small challenge for him, or at least that he's taking a lot longer to finish his meals than he used to. We occasionally change the composition of what he eats to include more or less vegetables, which are easier to chew and he seems to appreciate it. We also do the same with adding oatmeal to his meals, which—like for us humans—is a good and healthy item that also helps fill him up while being able to maintain his weight.

14 THE REST OF YOUR LIVES

I think this is the beginning of a beautiful friendship.

As a longtime movie buff, I love the final scene of the classic movie *Casablanca*, when the Captain says this line to Rick (played by Humphrey Bogart). Rick has basically lost everything, at the lowest point of his life, yet the uplifting connotations of that phrase is endless.

Your blind dog has similarly faced what seems like the lowest point of his life, which is now a life of darkness. And his biggest fear is that your love for him will be less, until he realizes that you bring him brightness; you are his seeing eye human.

You have taken a huge step in reading this book, and learning as much as you can about how to love and care for your blind dog. Perhaps you're reading this at the beginning of his journey, but it's also possible that you and he started his journey much earlier. Regardless of where you are on your journey with him, I hope the experiences I've shared in this book enable you to improve his confidence, give a sense of security in his quality of life, and empower you to let him know your love for him is unconditional.

The warrior spirit that I have repeatedly said Blackie has is his nature, perhaps standing firmly on the bond we have. His "never give up" attitude, similar to one displayed in Og Mandino's *The Twelfth Angel*, that I described in the chapter titled "Acceptance by your dog," motivates me every day to be there for him, with him. Your dog will (or perhaps already has) a similar warrior spirit, and your purpose in life must be to work with him through your unconditional love so that he continues to have a good quality of life. Sadly, dogs lead a much shorter life than us, so your journey with him will likely be until he heads toward that rainbow bridge, the fictional place where dogs go when they pass away and wait to be reunited with their owners. The rest of your lives together may seem short, so let him know you're there for him.

You are his ***seeing eye human!***

You have the ***superpower of observation*** to assist him in his journey.

He looks for ***total trust*** with you through his ***unconditional love*** for you!

And, finally, remember that ***your blind dog sees you through his heart.***

Appendix A: Hong Kong Dog Rescue (HKDR)

All profits from the sale of this book go to local dog rescue charities. For more information, including how you can help or adopt a dog in need of rescue in Hong Kong, go to: www.hongkongdogrescue.com. HKDR is the truly no-kill dog rescue operation in the Hong Kong.

Firstly, a special thanks to Sally Anderson, HKDR's founder and tireless leader. Sally is one of the key inspirations that led me to write the story of Blackie's journey in hopes of motivating others and helping them embrace the unconditional love that a blind dog has, rather than focusing on his or her adversity. Sally has woken up every day for over 20 years to save the lives of blind dogs, deaf dogs, disabled dogs, puppies, adult dogs, senior dogs, and any other abandoned dogs—healthy or otherwise—that she can find, in hopes of housing them until a loving family can adopt them.

About HKDR

HKDR was founded in 2003 for the specific purpose of saving dogs and puppies from the Hong Kong Government's Agriculture, Fisheries and Conservation Department (AFCD) Animal Management Centres, where thousands of dogs and puppies are destroyed every year. They are homeless and unwanted, and have just four days to live unless they are chosen for rehoming.

Although almost all HKDR dogs and puppies are still rescued from AFCD, these days many of their dogs are also ex-breeding dogs, those that are no longer useful for the purpose of producing puppies for the pet trade. These dogs are inevitably in poor health and condition due to their previous hard lives, and they need extensive veterinary treatment.

Only a small percentage of these dogs and puppies are lucky enough to be rescued by HKDR, after which the larger ones will be taken care of at their main Tai Po Homing Centre, while smaller dogs awaiting rehoming will stay at the Ap Lei Chau Homing Centre. Puppies usually live at the HKDR base on Lamma Island or stay in foster homes, and they are taken to Whiskers N Paws (a prominent and caring pet shop in Hong Kong) at Horizon Plaza, Ap Lei Chau, every Sunday afternoon where potential adopters can meet them and hopefully take them home.

As much as possible, puppies and smaller dogs are placed in temporary foster care where they can live in a home environment before being permanently adopted. HKDR's foster network plays a vital role in helping dogs overcome the trauma of being abandoned or their previous unhappy circumstances, such as those that are rescued from breeding farms.

Alongside the rescue and rehoming efforts, education is also an important part of HKDR's mission, and as part of that the Education & Training Centre was opened in July 2013. This small venue is used for a variety of workshops and classes, all of which are designed to help improve dog–human understanding and so reduce the number of pets being abandoned. Whiskers N Paws also hosts the HKDR "Positive Partners" Training Courses, which are designed to promote responsible pet ownership as well as reward-based training methods.

Donations help drive dedication

HKDR is funded almost entirely by private donations, with the addition of one-off grants, event sponsorship, merchandise sales, and fundraising events, with free desexing provided by AFCD for all dogs and puppies taken from their Animal Management Centres and an annual Subvention (amount varies). All of the dogs and puppies that HKDR take in for rehoming are health checked, vaccinated, given flea, tick, and heartworm prevention, and desexed. Those who require additional veterinary treatment or surgery are given the best available. Dogs with behavioral problems are rehabilitated using Positive Reinforcement training methods to make them ready for adoption.

HKDR relies heavily on the time and efforts of dedicated volunteers to be able to operate and many of the important functions of the organization are handled solely by such volunteers, such as their Foster and Life Saver Club programs, and even the Volunteer Coordination itself.

HKDR is proud to be a no-kill organization, meaning that no dog under their care will be euthanized for any reason other than when it is the only humane option.

Please visit the HKDR website and consider donating at: www.hongkongdogrescue.com.

Appendix B: Blackie's Life Story and Photo Gallery

Blackie came into our lives as a rescue dog from a local dog rescue operation on Lamma Island in Hong Kong. He was actually rescued by a friend in 2010, and the best guess of his birthday is December 3, 2008 … which is really only an arbitrary selection of the date "12-3" in late 2008. Although he was brown, my friend had named him Blackie because she already had a dog named Brownie (who was, of course, black).

Blackie (and Brownie) would frequently come to my house to socialize with my two dogs at that time, Angel and Jazmine. They all loved playing together, and Blackie and Angel quickly became best friends. However, Blackie never liked me in the early years and I could only surmise that he was abused by a man in his earlier life as he was incredibly cautious and defensive around any men. The fact is, it took me about two years to get Blackie to trust me enough to touch and pet him. Fortunately, however, throughout this time he was always happy and ready to walk with me and Angel.

Shortly after we started to get along, Blackie and Brownie moved into my house, changing our house status from two to four dogs, and making our "dog lover" house a "dog pack lover" house. We grew to a pack of five in the following year when another one-year-old rescue, Princess, followed the same friend down a mountain she was hiking and, fortunately, refused to abandon us. Over the next few years, Blackie and I— the only two boys in the house— gradually became closer and closer, eventually to that point of "total trust." While I would hate to say I had a favorite among the pack, Blackie, knowing he was my favorite boy, knew that Angel was my favorite overall. But the entire pack got along extremely well, and there were never any fights.

I retired in mid-2016 and began spending increased time with all of the pack. Our walks and hikes for three (Blackie, Angel, and I) changed to walks and hikes for four, with Princess joining or otherwise crying the entire time we were gone. The three of them loved, in particular, hiking the incredible mountain trails with me. I never walked or hiked with them on a leash, having trained them to appropriately obey commands to keep them out of harm's way. We were all close buddies.

In late November 2017, Blackie abruptly changed. At home, he suddenly became aggressive with the other dogs, primarily at feeding time. On our walks, he seemed not to want to go up the stairs to exit our house and wasn't able to adequately keep up on the walks, to the point that I started leaving him behind at home. We knew something had to be wrong.

In early December 2016, we started taking him to our local vet who did every test on him that she could— physicals, urine tests, blood tests, you name it. There were no signs of anything. I think she prescribed something for a potential upset stomach, which could have been a cause. Yes, she even checked his eyes and they looked normal (and still do). He also reacted normally to her touch. I think he was tested three times that month leading up to the Christmas holidays; the battery of tests revealed nothing.

But the aggressive behavior continued and worsened, so much so that we had to separate Blackie from the pack at feeding time and limit his walks with the other dogs. The holiday season set in and they weren't "Happy Holidays" knowing Blackie was experiencing something as yet unexplained. I ultimately started research of my own (with Google's assistance) through volumes of possible behavioral explanations. While I initially came across potential blindness, Blackie's eyes didn't give off any observational signs and he seemed to react to my motions as though he could see fine.

For example, I would previously say something like, "here's a treat," and toss it to him and he would be able to catch it. By all indications, he wasn't blind. Instead, I now took a treat, while remaining silent, and moved it around. However, he continued to follow my movements, with his beautiful eyes seemingly following the treat.

144

I was feeling tricked and finally decided I needed some innovative stimulation exercises to accurately evaluate his senses. I finally took a non-food item that looked like a treat but was cleansed of any smells. When I waved this in front of his line of sight, there was no movement or reaction. I tried the same on Angel and Princess, and their eyesight followed it like a missile locked on its target. I developed a few similar "tests" such as moving a piece of furniture just slightly, calling Blackie to me, and realizing he would walk into or bump it (but nothing harmful), and turning off all the lights in the event that he may be vision-impaired but could follow shadows and shades.

By removing the ability of his other senses to assist him, I was able to isolate that he was having a vision problem. When I had said "treat," he was switched on and, I'm convinced, listened for the sound of the treat being tossed, followed the smell of the treat and hoped he opened his mouth at the right time. Silly me, as I had a real good aim and had not made it too difficult for him. But once I effectively muted the ability of his other senses to guide him over three days of similar but varied tests, I was 99.9% sure he could be blind or at least vision-impaired.

On that third day (now in early January), I took him back to the vet and explained my theory, even demonstrated it for her. She again examined his eyes and reconfirmed no observational signs of eye disease, let alone blindness. However, she did say, "I think your assessment may be correct, but I have never seen this before." We immediately got Blackie an appointment with Hong Kong's top veterinary ophthalmologist, Dr. Derek Chow at Veterinary Specialty Hospital[14]. I already knew Dr. Chow, as he was treating Princess for a birth defect commonly known as "dry eyes."

The next morning, Dr. Chow performed a thorough and proper ophthalmology exam and gave us the bad news, that Blackie had SARDS. A thousand questions followed and the only bits of good news were that it's

---

[14] The Veterinary Specialty Hospital (VSH) of Hong Kong team and, in particular, Dr. Derek Chow, Veterinary Ophthalmologist, are amazing. For more information on VSH and Dr. Chow see vsh.com.hk.

not painful, and not life-threatening. That didn't lessen the devastation of knowing my boy Blackie had lost his sight forever … and the pain I felt for not being able to understand what he was going through for the past six weeks. I was ashamed. I had let my buddy down.

Imagine again what I described in the first paragraph of the introduction to this book, where you awaken tomorrow to discover you're blind, seeing nothing but darkness. Now try to imagine that you can't tell anyone for ten months (the dog equivalent of six weeks), while they try to figure out why you're behaving differently. I felt a huge burden and wasn't sure how or when it would ever be lifted.

When I got home, I picked up on the research that I'd been doing and was able to quickly start to put together a plan that ultimately led to the experiences I've shared in this book. I began spending every day, at least for the first few weeks, focused on how to help Blackie and effectively repent for my inability to understand what he was going through. My best guess is that it was about three months later (the dog equivalent of nearly three years) that the bond I had then formed with Blackie was clear: he trusted me again—"***total trust***" as I would say to him. His trust rescued me from the burden I had carried. He truly was forgiving and inspirational.

Along that part of the journey, his interest in playing catch grew enormously as it engaged his other senses during playtime: listening for the ball coming through the air, bouncing, and then letting the sniffer kick in to find it. Mind you, I wasn't tossing the ball far, and rarely more than about five or six feet, but he relished it. Interestingly, before going blind he had little interest in ever playing catch or fetch, but now he loved playing "ball." This is not uncommon among dogs that develop blindness.

Sadly, a few months later on August 2, 2018, an accident occurred leaving Blackie paralyzed with head trauma, and further diagnosis impractical until he could receive X-rays and an MRI. He was on an afternoon walk with the friend who had originally adopted him and a dog-walking helper, who tossed him the ball as usual. Unfortunately, Blackie headbutted the ball causing it to accelerate at a ninety-degree angle, and he took off dashing toward the sound of the ball bouncing. The result was running headfirst into a light post and immediately collapsing. He couldn't move. They picked up his paralyzed body and rushed him to the vet less than ten minutes away.

I was skydiving in Thailand when I got the call. I was in tears and feared the worst. I began making itinerary changes to rush to Bangkok and catch the next flight back to Hong Kong, which would be at about three in the morning. I headed to the airport immediately, hoping for the possibility of an earlier flight, which wasn't possible. I received another call, this time from the vet, saying that Blackie was in so much pain that I need to prepare myself for the possibility of putting him to sleep. I said, "no way!" I gave instructions to get him to Peace Avenue Veterinary Clinic (now known as CityU VMC)[15]—which I knew had a veterinary neurologist on staff—and into intensive care that evening, and to begin administering any pain management medicine as appropriate. When I arrived at six in the morning, I went straight to the hospital. I authorized X-rays and an MRI, and found Dr. Shanshan Guo[16], the Resident in Neurology, to take his case with a sense of urgency. Most importantly, I spent as much time with Blackie as the hospital's intensive care ward would allow, so that he could feel a sense of reassurance … his best friend was here to rescue him.

Dr. Guo diagnosed him (in my plain English, not in precise medical terms) as having a severely bruised spine and nervous system, but no broken bones. I asked her for his prospects of recovery and I recall

---

[15] For more information on Peace Avenue Veterinary Clinic in Hong Kong, which was renamed CityU Veterinary Medical Centre (aka CityU VMC) in April 2019, go to cityuvmc.com.hk.

[16] Dr. Shanshan Guo, the Resident in Neurology at CityU VMC is amazing. For more information about her, go to cityuvmc.com.hk.

her summarizing it as a 60% chance of recovery in about six months if he was not blind, which added tremendous complexity to his recuperation. I broke the good news to Blackie: "You're going to make it. I'm not sure how or when but you're going to make it." The look on his face was skeptical, but filled with total trust in me.

He spent the next two weeks in the hospital's intensive care ward, in part due to a mild build-up of liquid in his lungs. In the meantime, Blackie continued with pain management medication and I started on two priorities. First, I had made the decision to seek acupuncture treatments for him given the nature of the spinal injuries (further discussed below). Brownie, one of Blackie's older sisters, had undergone acupuncture to help with her hips as she was aging and I knew treatments could be successful. Second, I knew I had to be there for my buddy whenever I could, which in intensive care meant three times a day for thirty minutes during the hospital's visiting windows: 6:30am, 1:30pm, and 8:00pm.

Despite the hospital being an hour-and-a-half commute each way from my home, I only missed about three sessions and then only because my friend (Blackie's original adopter) visited instead. I was there every morning for him at 6:30am. This poor guy must have struggled through each night, listening to the cries of other dogs, laying there blind and paralyzed in his world of darkness, worried about whether he had been abandoned. No way! I couldn't bear the thought of that, and had to be there every morning. While many dog owners know the feeling of elation their dogs may exhibit when they return home from even a short trip away, with some dogs jumping excitedly, a greater feeling is seeing your blind and paralyzed dog on the verge of giving up at dawn but then his ears perk up (that sense of sound) to my normal call and his face starts to brighten up with his dog smile, while the rest of his body simply cannot move. What made it even more special for Blackie was that every single day I was there, none of the other intensive care patients had any visitors during that early morning visiting window. It took a couple of days, but Blackie understood this, and despite his life-threatening injury on top of his blindness, he knew he was special. I think he came to expect me each morning, part of our "total trust" bond.

Interestingly, I observed the varying number of intensive care patients during Blackie's stay (generally between ten and twenty) and estimated that for the 1:30pm visiting window only about a third of the dogs had visitors, while for the evening session only about two-thirds had visitors. Blackie had a visitor for 100% of the visiting windows while he was there.

By the time Blackie was released to come home (still paralyzed), he was no longer skeptical. Total trust! He knew I was there to rescue him, while I knew he would warrior his way through this.

Seeking acupuncture treatments, however, was no easy task. Our community on a somewhat remote island didn't have any resident veterinarians skilled in acupuncture. I visited perhaps twenty such veterinarians throughout Hong Kong, pleading for house calls three times a week for the indefinite future. No luck with house calls. However, I found Tin Hau Pet Hospital ("THPH") about an hour away from home that specialized in acupuncture treatments and traditional Chinese medicine[17]. The entire team at THPH were wonderful, with a special call out to Dr. Angela Yung and Christy Lee, one of the nurses there who patiently helped nurture Blackie three times a week for about three months, after which this reduced to two times a week and eventually once a week as Blackie regained his ability to move. I'd like to give an additional shout out to THPH's entire staff, who on one day or another also assisted with treating Blackie. He was rescued from this traumatic injury over about a five-month period, altering the statistics underlying that 60% chance in six months prognosis that Dr. Guo had given (with no disrespect to her as another outstanding and crucial member of Blackie's recovery team). My boy Blackie was back, albeit with the need to permanently cut out playing ball.

---

[17] The entire team at THPH is amazing, especially Dr. Angela Yung and nurse Christy Lee, who were the primary caregivers for Blackie's acupuncture treatments. For more information about THPH, go to thph.com.hk.

Fresh from his warrior victory in beating the paralysis, Blackie contracted tick fever. I'm still puzzled by this, as his exposure outside the home was so limited in comparison to the rest of the pack, yet none of the rest of them got it. Nevertheless, with his warrior spirit intact, and the help of appropriate medicines, he also kicked tick fever in April 2019. If only every dictionary on this earth could show a picture of Blackie for the definition of "inspirational."

Blackie began adjusting to his new life as a blind dog unable to play ball, while the rest of the pack tried to understand their new normal as well. Dog lovers will be the first to testify that dogs do have and show feelings. This was truly the case in my house with each of the pack members learning how to live with and treat Blackie, perhaps not as a handicap (such a derogatory word) but with dignity as a less-fortunate member of the pack. Most notable, however, was that Angel's reaction by this time had become one of jealousy, but not malicious jealousy. Simply put, Angel had become jealous of the extra time and attention

Blackie got from me and began to distance herself a bit from him. The remedy, of course, was that I needed and did spend more alone time with Angel, as well as ensuring that Angel, Princess, and I still got our exhausting hikes in on a frequent basis. Angel passed away suddenly of kidney disease in early 2019, and I can also tell that Blackie missed her, as did the rest of the pack. On two different occasions, I am certain that I saw Princess crying shortly after Angel's sudden and unexpected departure, which was not easy for a dog with a dry eyes condition.

Although my own grief was severe, I again felt rescued by Blackie who tried to fill the emotional gap that Angel's passing had created. He knew he would have a little more of my attention. Yes, he had rescued me again. This continued well into 2020 until the next challenge arose.

In early 2020, Blackie was diagnosed with the potential onset of kidney disease. But it was early stage and only required monitoring of his nutrition as well as frequent blood tests and the "markers" for his kidney and liver. In late August, not too long after his last round of blood tests, he suddenly lost his appetite and was drinking excessively. It only took a few days to see it, and I rushed him to the vet for another battery of tests. Unfortunately, on August 31, 2020, he was diagnosed with very severe Stage 4 kidney disease with a prediction that he would live only one to two weeks. I again said, "no way!"

Blackie initially started a round of intravenous fluids treatment ("IVFT") on daily visits to the vet. I had made a deliberate decision initially that the benefit of him sleeping at home each night, which meant he would only have about eight hours of IVFT daily while at the vet, outweighed the benefits of confining him to a hospital even though he would get closer to 24 hours of IFVT daily. His quality of life would have been nil. I firmly believe it was the right decision as he was able to maintain high spirits and good energy but after a couple of days, an updated blood test showed signs of further deterioration.

Instead, I immediately set out to purchase an IVFT monitor for at-home use, so that I could have him on the IVFT essentially full time but in the comfort of our home. His home. The first challenge was that while Blackie's vet agreed with it being a good strategy, they could neither loan nor sell us an IVFT monitor for legal reasons. The second challenge was finding a supplier to sell me one, since I'm not a vet myself. The third challenge, once I found the first supplier, was a seven-day waiting period. No way! I persisted and found another supplier, and was quickly able to set up the IVFT monitor at home.

While aiming for 24 hours per day of IVFT, the reality was that, after considering some periodic breaks including short and energizing walks, this amounted to about 18-20 hours per day. Within a few days (and sleepless nights) he started to show tremendous improvement, and an updated blood test at the two-week date revealed that his markers showed improvements compared to his initial diagnosis, although still within Stage 4. Subsequent blood tests showed he was, in general terms, stable. Blackie was truly a warrior with a will to live.

This rescue continued as I sat down to write this book. On the verge of losing my best friend, I knew our story had to be told and shared so that others with blind dogs can take up the call to be a seeing eye human, as I had. Stories and tips had to be distilled while he was still here, so that I could let him know that his life had more meaning than just being my best friend, although that's all he ever asked for with his unconditional love.

For the next month, Blackie continued to remain relatively stable, followed by the inevitable deterioration that we knew would come. Thus, about six weeks after he was given one to two weeks to live, he lost his appetite and our ability to keep him on sustained IVFT was challenged by the need to find a new vein in which to connect his IVFT. With IVFT, the catheter location needs to be rotated every few days, but doing this causes scarring of the veins, which—when coupled with a decline in blood pressure—make finding a useful vein like fishing for catfish in a nearly empty lake; you drop your line in because you know there are fish there even though you can't see them, and you may hook a few but have trouble reeling them in. Finding new and sufficiently healthy vein locations resulted in a few periods of no IVFT so that his veins could recuperate. The signs were increasing that his organs were shutting down, but he still had his ever-present "no way" and "never give up" attitude.

As we knew the end was nearing, I had a lot of additional discussions with my Blackie, my warrior and my inspiration. I reminded him of the good times we shared before he was blind, and the many great times we'd had since. I also kept reminding him to not be in a hurry to get to that rainbow bridge[18], while

---

[18] According to Wikipedia (wikipedia.org/wiki/Rainbow_Bridge_(pets)), the rainbow bridge is the theme of several works of poetry written in the 1980s and 1990s that speak of an other-worldly place where pets go upon death, eventually to be reunited with their owners. One is a prose poem whose original creator is uncertain. The other is a six-stanza poem of rhyming pentameter couplets, created by a couple to help ease the pain of friends who lost pets. Each has gained popularity around the world among animal lovers who have lost a pet or a wild animal that are cared for. The belief has many antecedents, including similarities to the Bifröst bridge of Norse mythology.

also giving him a list of the things for him to tell Angel, among the others that had passed before him. Blackie was always at peace that Angel *was* my favorite, but he knew that in the present day, he *is* my favorite.

On the evening of November 2, 2020, we saw that it was time. Blackie was still fighting; he didn't want to leave me. I gave him comforting words, telling him it was time to surrender peacefully, and hoped he would during the night. The problem is that Blackie simply doesn't have any type of white flag within him with which to surrender.

Morning came, and we knew he needed our help as he was now crying, in unbearable pain, and the prospects for any quality of life were gone. We arranged for his vet to come to our house at lunchtime and assist him.

We prepared an area in our backyard on that sunny and comfortably cool afternoon, surrounded by us, his original rescuer, his sister dogs Jazmine and Princess, and a couple other dog friends he had. The setting for his final minutes was one of his favorite places, surrounded by friends and family.

While waiting for the vet to arrive, I laid face-to-face with Blackie whispering my profound thanks to him for being in my life. I reiterated that I would tell our story so that other blind dogs could have a better quality of life, and that other people, like myself, could be blessed with the opportunity to be a seeing eye human. He smiled and, at one point, he looked at me eye-to-eye and I thought, for a split second, that his vision was back and he was perhaps trying to take a final earthly look at his best friend. I can never be sure whether his sight was suddenly and momentarily back as we said our goodbyes, but I am certain that he saw me with his heart. Blind dogs truly see with their hearts.

Rest in peace, Blackie. One of the magical aspects of reaching the other side of that rainbow bridge is that all of your struggles are gone. I know you can see and run around and play with Angel and your other friends, and sharing with them the great times we had together. Thank you for everything you did for me, and the times we shared. I love you deeply, and I will, in fact, tell our story.

Summary of Blackie's overall life journey

Date	Event in Blackie's overall life journey
December 3, 2008	Best guess of Blackie's birthday as "12-3", 2008.
2010	Adopted by our friend, and came into our lives but would not accept anything to do with me.
2012	Moved into my house.
2012 / 2013	Blackie started to like me—the beginning of total trust.
2013–2017	The good years.
November 2017	Blackie contracted SARDS, but could not tell us.
January 2018	Blackie formally diagnosed with SARDS.
January–April 2018	Our lives changed to accommodate Blackie.
August 2, 2018	Blackie ran headfirst into a light post, with resulting head trauma causing paralysis.
August 2018– February 2019	Blackie's recuperation period involving acupuncture, traditional Chinese medicine, and lots of love and caring.
March / April 2019	Blackie contracts tick fever.
Early 2020	Blackie diagnosed with potential onset of kidney disease.
August 31, 2020	Blackie diagnosed with very severe Stage 4 kidney disease with a prognosis that he would live only one to two weeks.
November 3, 2020	Blackie crossed the rainbow bridge.

Some of the author's favorite photos of Blackie with him and his "sisters," each of which recalls a special memory.

Appendix C: Other Resources

As mentioned in various places throughout this book, the best advice when trying to learn how to love and care for a blind dog is to learn as much as possible, both at the beginning and throughout the rest of your dog's life. Other resources that the author found very useful include the following:

The Internet – Relentless research by Googling every possible question.

Books – There are many books with authors that share similar experiences, but the two that the author found the most helpful are *My Blind Dog Still Wags His Tail* by J.D. Wilcock, *My dog is blind but still lives life to the full!* by Nicole Horsky, and *Walking in Trust: Lessons I Learned with my Blind Dog* by Gayle M. Irwin (who also has many other great dog stories).

Friends and fellow dog lovers – Talk to as many friends and fellow dog lovers as possible, because even those that don't have a blind dog may know someone who does.

Vets – Talk to your dog's veterinarian and ask for their advice but also ask about connecting with other people who have or had blind dogs.

Veterinary ophthalmologist – As much as you wouldn't only speak to a family doctor if you were blind, do your best to speak with a veterinary ophthalmologist for a diagnosis, treatment, and—most importantly—connecting you with other people who have or had blind dogs. The cost of a visit is well worth what you can learn about loving and caring for your blind dog.

Appendix D: Tips from Blackie's Journey

I hope you've enjoyed the various stories I've shared about experiences with my blind Blackie as we traveled through his journey of darkness together with unconditional love for each other. If you have gotten this far in this book, I have no doubt you've fully embraced the knowledge of your **superpower** of observation, and the warmth achieved when you incorporate the ***Magical Eight Modifiers*** into building—or rebuilding—a new sense of ***total trust***.

The following summary index of those "Tips from Blackie's Journey" may help you to refer to one or more of them more easily from time to time.

Tip from Blackie's journey	Synopsis
1. The slightest sounds *From page 31, Open your eyes*	Learn early how to use your superpower of observation, even for simple tasks that your blind dog has done for many years, such as the sounds he may hear while performing those tasks.

Tip from Blackie's journey	Synopsis
2. Show a little dignity *From page 32,* *Open your eyes*	Through my superpower of observation, I noticed that some members of our five-dog pack did this, while others did not. We learned to observe the other dogs when Blackie would move around as it became important to alert Angel or Princess to "be nice" in order to avoid any confrontations. Eventually Angel and Princess also learned to adapt; they, too, just needed time to adjust to Blackie's new norms.
3. Ding, ding, ding *From page 57,* *Use of a bell*	Hanging a bell on your blind dog's collar is a good way to know when he is on the move.
4. The water bowl location *From page 58,* *Sounds and smells*	Listen and learn what your blind dog is hearing and whether something needs to be modified (e.g. the location of his water bowl) to encourage a particular behavior.
5. Praise, even for finding the water bowl *From page 59,* *Sounds and smells*	Using positive praise even for small successes reinforces his feeling of safety and helps to give him more confidence.
6. Muting competing sounds *From page 60,* *Sounds and smells*	Recognize that your blind dog's acute hearing hears all various sounds. Muting competing sounds is helpful when he's learning things or mapping his home. Music can be a comforting background noise, particularly when he is left alone.

Tip from Blackie's journey	Synopsis
7. Anxiety at feeding time *From page 61, Sounds and smells*	Anxiety at feeding time is normal for a blind dog. Talk to your dog as you prepare his meal. If you have other pets, separate them at feeding time.
8. The two-handed head-to-head squeeze *From page 65, Touching*	Touching your blind dog can be one of the best rewards you can give him. Experiment and find out how your blind dog likes to be touched (or even hugged) that gives him the most comforting feeling of love and security.
9. No biting *From page 69, No scolding, and hitting must be rare*	Don't scold your blind dog for bad behaviors as his heightened sense of hearing and focus on your tone can cause more anxiety. Hitting should be rare or non-existent as it, and negative tones, cause significant anxiety. Reprimand and teach your blind dog in a calming voice as your dog knows when he hasn't been a good boy, and never call him a "bad boy." In particular, any biting behaviors need to be corrected in a way that builds on his "total trust."
10. Feeding bowl location *From page 72, Feeding*	Ensure that his feeding bowl location allows him to move around and not bump into things while enjoying his meal.
11. Time to drink *From page 72, drinking*	Recognize that a "drink" command or the sound of water being put in his bowl or tapping on the bowl can be good acoustic ways to use his sense of hearing to prompt him to drink.

Tip from Blackie's journey	Synopsis
12. Doody time *From page 73,* *Going potty*	Help your blind dog with his mapping of where he should go potty, both in the garden—if you have one—and any other locations outside your house. Consider using doggie wipes to cleans his paws when he returns into the house to promote good hygiene as blind dogs often inadvertently step in their urine.
13. Bells in the night *From page 75,* *Sleeping*	Hanging a bell on your blind dog's collar is also good way (if you are a light enough sleeper) to know when he is on the move during the night.
14. Favorite chill spots *From page 76,* *Hanging out /* *Resting*	Learn the spots in your house where your blind dog can just relax in comfort, particularly when no one else is at home. Recognize that your blind dog's acute hearing may focus on certain sounds in one location more than in another. Your blind dog may also have more than one spot where he likes to just hang out and rest.
15. Who put that there? *From page 83,* *Mapping*	Mapping is your blind dog's way of knowing his world of darkness. If someone moves something or places something in his mapped paths, he will try to update his maps, which are only effective as long as the routes don't change.

Tip from Blackie's journey	Synopsis
16. The sound of silence *From page 85, Sounds*	Unexpected sounds can quickly cause anxiety in your blind dog. When rain (and possibly thunder) is forecast overnight, we leave some sound playing—even at a much lower level—to soothe the effect of those unexpected noises that may startle him from the sound of silence.
17. Lemon juice drops *From page 86, Smells and scenting*	Placing uniquely identifiable but not harmful scents in the house is an innovative way to use your blind dog's primary scent of smell to locate obstacles, such as doorways and steps. We used lemon juice drops for our doorways until Blackie had these fully mapped, after which we stopped.
18. Vanilla not chocolate steps *From page 87, Stairs*	We used drops of vanilla extract to help Blackie our steps by placing a few on a small rug strips placed at the top and bottom of each staircase. We continue to do this, as a blind dog naturally has some level of anxiety when it comes to stairs.

Tip from Blackie's journey	Synopsis
19. Bumper cars are fun; bumper dogs are not *From page 89, Guards and bumpers*	Some furniture may have cornered edges at or near your blind dog's head or body height. You can place rubber guards or bumpers on these cornered edges to that your dog can more safely bump into them without causing injury or anxiety, knowing he is safe around the home. In Blackie's case, I also observed that a square-shaped wooden bed post on his path to a particular staircase would cause him to "freeze" in his tracks, another sign of anxiety. We took a thick bath towel and wrapped it around the bed post. Success! Total trust restored.
20. "Step" and "down" *From page 93, Old and new commands*	Blackie has been re-taught that "up" can be used for going up steps, but he has been taught the new command "step" when going down steps / curbs / uneven surfaces to avoid confusion with his existing understanding of what "down" meant. We consistently guide him down all steps with our hands and clearly and repeatedly say "step" for each and every step downward. A praiseful "good" or "good boy" to reinforce the proper behavior usually follows each step for his sense of security.

Tip from Blackie's journey	Synopsis
21. No no no *From page 94, Old and new command*	Dogs understand that "no" distinctly means to not do something. Using the word "no" around a blind dog will immediately cause confusion for him because he can't see if you are speaking to him or to another dog or person. We taught him the command "no no no", which is used only for Blackie. We say it in a monotone voice without any tonal emphasis so that it comes across as a safety or—in the case of our walks—corrective command, rather than a disciplinary or otherwise negative command that may cause anxiety.
22. His first steps as an angel *From page 98, Halo harness*	A halo harness can be the most successful aid employed in helping your blind dog gain confidence to move freely when outside (and possibly inside if your home is spacious enough).
23. The root of the problem *From page 101, Safe and fun walking routes*	Momentary lapses in observing your blind dog may result in his tripping over something unexpectedly, such as protruding tree roots. Keep your superpower of observation on even though you and him may have trekked those safe and fun walking routes many times.
24. Smell the roses *From page 103, Vary the routine*	With his acute sense of smell, varying his routine walks allows him to lose himself in the abundance of new and differing smells he picks up.

Tip from Blackie's journey	Synopsis
25. He likes to watch *From page 106, Playtime*	Blind dogs can enjoy being around other dogs that are playing as they effectively watch with their primary sense of hearing. Ensuring your dog experiences these interactions can energize him even if can't participate himself.
26. Multiple accessories *From page 111, Blind dog alert collars*	Accessorizing your blind dog with a collar, harness and / or leash that says "BLIND DOG" is a great way to announce to an approaching person that your dog is blind. This is particularly useful when that person is walking their own dog, as it can create a helpful reminder to be cautious when socializing.
27. Let me help you smell her *From page 120, How dogs socialize*	Help your blind dog avoid the way-too-quick rear-end sniffing encounters with other dogs and soothe his anxiety by talking with and petting the other dog, then sharing the other dog's scent on your hand with your blind dog. Encourage people you meet to have them offer the back of their hand to your blind dog to smell them, which also eases their anxiety in meeting people (both old and new friends).

Tip from Blackie's journey	Synopsis
28. A little too excitable *From page 121,* *How dogs socialize*	You can't predict reliably how another dog may provoke your blind dog, particularly dogs that have an exuberant liveliness well past the puppy stage of their life. Keep your superpower of observation on even though your blind dog may have known the other dog for many years and the two have played together many times before he went blind.
29. Blackie's big sister *From page 125,* *Other household dogs*	Other dogs in the household may act as a companion for a blind dog and be of great benefit, literally becoming the dog's own "seeing eye dog". If you're considering adding another four-legged companion into your house, consider fostering a rescue dog to first assess the compatibility of the new household member with your blind dog.
30. Meal choices *From page 132,* *Aging*	Consider the extent of proper nutrition and possible use of supplements as your blind dog ages. Blind dogs tend to have lower levels of exercise as compared with the levels of sighted dogs. His aging is inevitable, but you can help him avoid nutritional deficiencies that may unexpectedly arise as a result of his lifestyle as a blind dog.

Appendix E: Acknowledgements

Firstly, a big thanks to all of the professionals that helped us care for Blackie since he was stricken with blindness, including Dr. Derek Chow at VSH; Drs. Joanne Harries, Isabella Luk, and Jonette Dimblad at Discovery Bay Pet Space; Dr. Shanshan Guo at CityU VMC; Dr. Angela Yung and Christy Lee at THPH; and all of their extended staff.

Secondly, thanks to my and Blackie's family and friends who shared our journey, especially Brownie, Angel, Jazmine, Princess, and Olivia.

Lastly, thanks to Blackie for rescuing me throughout our journey together. I miss you buddy, but I will see you again someday. In the meantime, enjoy the sights across the rainbow bridge as you play with Brownie, Angel, and Olivia.

Appendix F: About the Author

Bob with Angel (who crossed the rainbow bridge in February 2019)

Bob Partridge resides in Hong Kong, where he's a
retired senior partner of EY (the global Big Four
consulting firm formerly known as Ernst & Young).
His professional career brought him from the United
States to Hong Kong, where he co-founded a
consulting practice across the Asia-Pacific region
specializing in mergers and acquisitions. Bob is a
former United States Marine Corps Drill Instructor

and Tank Commander, an avid skydiver, paraglider, and rescue dog lover, while always questioning the rescue dog relationship: *who rescues who?*

His first rescue dog, Angel, was from HKDR and rescued him years before Blackie came along. Angel went on to help Bob change his lifestyle to include a fitness regimen primarily centered around walking with Angel and his other dogs; his pack was comprised of five dogs for many years. Bob credits Angel for helping him lose 100 pounds (~45kg) in seven months and keeping it off (forever) through a life-changing sustainable transformation he made that is the subject of a forthcoming inspirational book.

All profits from this book are donated to local dog charities including Hong Kong Dog Rescue (HKDR). Please go to hongkongdogrescue.com to see how you can donate to HKDR, Hong Kong's truly no-kill rescue operation.

www.peartreebooks.com

Stay connected with Bob and his other books at:

www.peartreebooks.com.

Printed in Great Britain
by Amazon